COWLEY PUBLICATIONS is a ministry of the brothers of the Society of Saint John the Evangelist, a monastic order in the Episcopal Church. Our mission is to provide books and resources for those seeking spiritual and theological formation. COWLEY PUBLICATIONS is committed to developing a new generation of writers and teachers who will encourage people to think and pray in new ways about spirituality, reconciliation, and the future.

T0168097

Pathways to Peace

Interreligious Readings and Reflections

A. Jean Lesher, Editor

COWLEY PUBLICATIONS
CAMBRIDGE, MASSACHUSETTS

Library of Congress Cataloging-in-Publication Data

Interreligious reflections on pathways to peace
    Pathways to peace : interreligious readings and reflections / A. Jean Lesher, editor.
        p. cm.
    Includes bibliographical references and index.
    ISBN 1-56101-231-9 (pbk. : alk. paper)   I.   Peace—Religious aspects—Meditations.
    I. Lesher, A. Jean.   II. Title.
    BL65.P4I59 2005
    201'.7273—dc22   2005009449

Cover design: Gary Ragaglia

This book was printed in the United States of America on acid-free paper.

Cowley Publications
4 Brattle Street
Cambridge, Massachusetts 02138
800-225-1534 • www.cowley.org

Grateful acknowledgment is made to the following for permission to reprint material included in this book:

Alfred A. Knopf, Inc. (New York) for "Mother in Wartime" from THE COLLECTED POEMS OF LANGSTON HUGHES by Langston Hughes, copyright ©1994 by The Estate of Langston Hughes. Used by permission of Alfred A. Knopf, a division of Random House, Inc.

Central Conference of American Rabbis (CCAR Press, NY) for excerpts from *Gates of Repentance: The New Union Prayerbook for the Days of Awe.* Chaim Stern, Editor. Copyright 1996.

Doubleday (New York) for "Prayer for a Nuclear Age" from *A Cry for Mercy: Prayers from the Genesee* by Henri J. M. Nouwen, copyright 1981 by Henri J. M. Nouwen. Used by permission of Doubleday, a division of Random House, Inc.

Foundation for a Global Community (Palo Alto, CA) for an excerpt from an essay by Russell Schweickart in *Beyond War.* Copyright 1986.

New Directions Publishing Corp. (New York) for "Making Peace" by Denise Levertov, from BREATHING THE WATER, copyright ©1987 by Denise Levertov. Reprinted by permission of New Directions Publishing Corp.

New World Library (Novato, CA) for excerpts from essays by Mahnaz Afkhami, Jimmy Carter, Nadja Halibegovich, and Mother Teresa in *Architects of Peace: Visions of Hope in Words and Images.* Photography by Michael Collopy. Edited by Michael Collopy and Jason Gardner. Copyright 2000.

This book is dedicated to

Dirk Ficca

*untiring advocate for
international, interreligious
harmony*

Table of Contents

Introduction

Religion can be a realm of extraordinary power. It can offer solace in troubled times. It can make sense of the seemingly senseless because that's the world we live in. It can give us strength to meet the physical and spiritual challenges of life. Religion helps us find our place in the cosmos; it knits families and communities together; it endows individuals with compassion and morality. Whether one believes without question or wrestles with doubt, whether one is part of a religious community or worships in the privacy of the soul, religious practices and beliefs are among the phenomena that define us as human. For many of us, the axiom could well be: "We pray, therefore, we are."

(Kofi Annan, UN Secretary-General, The Millennium World Peace Summit of Religious and Spiritual Leaders, August 2000)

There will be no peace among the nations without peace among the religions.

(Hans Küng, co-author of "Towards a Global Ethic" for the Parliament of the World's Religions, 1993)

Few characteristics of the religions of the world are more common to all than the practices of praying and meditating. Communing with or appealing to that which is holy is as old as humankind and varied as the individuals and cultures involved. Some believers build temples for sacred rites; others prefer mountaintops or sacred groves; still others create little roadside shrines or designate caves as holy places for praying or meditating. Some prefer the privacy of bedsides or home altars.

Meditation rituals are observed in all faiths—repeating ancient chants at certain times or in certain places, turning prayer wheels, fingering prayer beads, touching holy objects, venerating sacred icons and statues, anointing the sick or dying, and lighting candles. The understanding of what is "the ultimate" or transcendent in life may be quite different, but the human need to address whatever is behind the many names used—be it God, Brahman, Allah, Great

Spirit, Holy One, perhaps "Mystery"—is common. Other believers seek to access an "inner spark of the divine."

Ancient sacred scriptures passed down through oral tradition were primarily concerned with personal well-being—how to lead a virtuous life or what rules a believer should follow to be faithful to the Master's teachings. Scribes for the world religions often recorded stories or parables that taught about responsible or faithful ways to live. These writings were less about the common good—especially what we now think of as global good—because scribes came from periods in history when a tribe was one's family and other tribes were enemies.

In today's global village, the religious imperative is to understand sacred texts in broader terms while remaining faithful to the intent of revered founders. We must seek passages that go beyond the personal and express concern for others, or we will not long survive in this new and threatening age. Such passages are available to us and need to become better known if world peace is to prevail.

In her introduction to a collection of prayers, Karen Armstrong, a distinguished commentator on religion, wrote: "All the great teachers of spirituality in all the major traditions have . . . insisted that before you can have faith, you must live in a certain way. You must lead a compassionate life, transcending the demands of the clamorous ego and recognizing the sacred in others; you must perform rituals (often enshrined in religious law) that make even the most mundane detail of our lives an encounter with the ultimate; all traditions insist that you must also pray. Prayer is thus not born of belief and intellectual conviction; it is a practice that creates faith" (*Every Eye Beholds You*). Swiss theologian Karl Barth wrote: "To clasp hands in prayer is the beginning of an uprising against the disorder of the world."

This book is a collection of readings from many religions, ages, and cultures. They are intended to enable peacemakers to recognize the common teachings in all religions—ancient and contemporary—that can bring us together for the global good.

Selections in *Pathways to Peace* can inspire faith communities to remember ancient cries for peace arising from all lands and ages during times of conflict and war. Modern technologies have created weapons that can destroy whole cities, civilizations, and even the earth itself. Pleas that peace will prevail on earth are coming with ever increasing frequency and with great and legitimate fear wherever and whenever aggressions appear. People can gain courage and strength through prayer and meditation to guide their responses at times of crises. The maintenance of peace in this world cannot be left to political and military leaders. International and interreligious organizations working for global peace are attracting millions who seek ways to stop the violence they witness in their communities and nations. Sant Rajinder Singh, president of the World Fellowship of Religions, spoke to 100,000 participants in a peace march in Delhi, India, in 1994, urging "people of all religions and faiths through universal meditation and prayer" to seek methods that will lead to world peace.

The selections in this book quoting from the sacred scriptures of major religions come from anthologies of translations previously chosen as important and eloquent writings. English translators of these texts from ancient languages tried to make them meaningful to contemporary readers. Their work can be seen as a significant contribution to interreligious respect for diverse spiritual writings. Comparatively modern writings are from well-known authors, world leaders, and organizations whose words express a religious under-standing of the theme of world peace.

I want to express deep appreciation to my contacts in the inter-religious and editorial worlds for their willingness to review early drafts of this book: Paul Chaffee, Lucy Kolin, Bill Lesher, Nancy Nielson, Alice Peppler, Helen Specter, and Heng Sure.

In October of each year, religious groups from many lands and all continents support the Week of Prayer for World Peace with special observances. Out of international, interfaith gatherings over many years has come the Universal Prayer for Peace (adapted from an ancient Jain chant):

> Lead me from death to life;
> from falsehood to truth.
> Lead me from despair to hope;
> from fear to trust.
> Lead me from hate to love;
> from war to peace.
> Let peace fill our heart,
> Our world, our universe.

The readings that follow are divided into three chapters corresponding to lines in the Universal Prayer for Peace. One can meditate on these and gain strength to participate in the unfolding dream of global peace.

A. Jean Lesher, Editor

Lead Me from Despair to Hope

There are many reasons for believing that deadly conflict among people is inevitable and little evidence that human behavior can be channeled toward the common good—especially on a global basis.

And yet—and yet—each baby born is God's "yes" to the future. Each morning is a new beginning; each spring overwhelms the decay of winter; each act of kindness kindles another.

St. John Climacus, an early Christian saint from what is now Palestine, wrote: "Prayer is the mother and daughter of tears. It is an expiation of sin, a bridge across temptation, a bulwark against affliction. It wipes out conflict, is the work of angels, and is the nourishment of everything spiritual" (*The Ladder of Divine Ascent*).

The readings that follow are intended to help lift up our spirits for the arduous journey from despair to hope on the path to peace.

Yom Kippur, which means "Day of Atonement," completes a penitential season in the Jewish calendar called "The Days of Awe." As described in the Hebrew Scriptures (Leviticus 16), it marks God's judgment upon the sins of all people and also God's forgiveness of humanity.

We cannot pray to You, O God, to banish war, for You have filled the world with paths to peace, if only we would take them.

We cannot pray to You to end starvation, for there is food enough for all, if only we would share it.

We cannot merely pray for prejudice to cease, for we might see the good in all that lies before our eyes, if only we would use them.

We cannot merely pray, "Root out despair," for the spark of hope already waits within the human heart, for us to fan it into flame.

We must not ask of You, O God, to take the task that You have given us. We cannot shirk, we cannot flee away, avoiding obligation for ever.

Therefore we pray, O God, for wisdom and will, for courage to do and to become, not only to look on with helpless yearning as though we had no strength.

For Your sake and ours, speedily and soon, let it be that our land may be safe, that our lives may be blessed.

May our words be pleasing in Your sight; may our deeds be acceptable to You, O God, our rock and our Redeemer.

(Stern, ed., Gates of Repentance)

Nadja Halilbegovich was a young Muslim girl in wartime Bosnia when she wrote in a diary about her experiences in war and close calls with death from bombings. Her diaries were published in Bosnia and Turkey and she became a well-known radio and concert singer in Europe and North America.

The war mercilessly stole four years of my life. Like every child would do, I acclimated to the new conditions of my life, forgetting what I had before. Every tear that stained my pillow at night, when all I could hear were sirens and grenades, was also a tear that mourned all the innocent citizens who lost their lives.

I often felt sad because the war opened my eyes at such an early age. Even though I learned a great lesson, sometimes it hurt so bad that I wish I had never learned it. Only my dreams, so beautiful that they could resist all the ugliness of war, so invulnerable that no grenades ever harmed them, kept my head and my hopes bright and high. I realized that the soft and colorful paths of my dreams often intersected with the roads of cruel reality. That was when my dreams, my determination, and my faith were tested.

War taught me that every human being has a dark and bright side. It is our choice to fight the darker side and show our warm and beautiful feelings or to let ourselves be weak and hopeless, bitter and mean. I hope that the warm and brilliant colors of the morning dawn, the radiant light of midnight's stars on the sky of my dreams will always light up my soul with goodness and faith. I hope they will light the path of my existence with peace and righteousness.

(quoted in Collopy, ed., *Architects of Peace*)

Pulitzer-prize–winning reporter for the New York Times, *Chris Hedges has been a foreign correspondent for more than twenty years, covering major conflicts in the Balkans, Africa, and the Middle East. This selection illustrates the notion that war can usurp religion in providing purpose—a ground for despair in modern times. These words are excerpted from Hedges's book* War Is a Force that Gives Us Meaning.

I learned early on that war forms its own culture. The rush of battle is a potent and often lethal addiction, for war is a drug, one I ingested for many years. It is peddled by myth makers—historians, war correspondents, filmmakers, novelists and the state—all of whom endow it with qualities it often does possess: excitement, exoticism, power, chances to rise above our small stations in life, and a bizarre and fantastic universe that has a grotesque and dark beauty. It dominates culture, distorts memory, corrupts language and infects everything around it, even humor, which becomes preoccupied with the grim perversities of smut and death.

Fundamental questions about the meaning, or meaninglessness, of our place on the planet are laid bare when we watch those around us sink to the lowest depths. War exposes the capacity for evil that lurks just below the surface within all of us.

An internationally recognized anthropologist and researcher on human evolution, Loren Eiseley (1908–1977) is best known for his book The Immense Journey, *which combined science and humanism. This quotation was taken from his autobiography* All the Strange Hours.

The need is not really for more brains, the need is now for a gentler, more tolerant people than those who won for us against the ice, the tiger, and the bear. The hand that hefted the ax, out of some old blind allegiance to the past, fondles the machine gun as lovingly. It is a habit humans will have to break to survive, but the roots go very deep.

This statement (here abridged) was read at the Central Ceremony of Interfaith Prayer for Peace in Santiago, Chile, September 2003, culminating a three-day observance in churches, schools, and communities.

We, representatives and members of diverse religions and spiritual traditions, are gathered today at the Headquarters of the United Nations in Santiago, to testify with our common prayer our commitment to the cause of peace and our will to live in harmony, mutually respecting our religious options and pursuing through dialogue common paths to build a new society more just, solidarian and fraternal than the present one. . . .

We want the Third Millennium we are starting to be more luminous than the previous one, which knew of horrible wars, genocides, colonialism, intolerance and religious persecution. We want for us, our children and the future generations a world where cultural and religious diversity will be respected and appreciated; a world of brothers and sisters reconciled among them and with the Earth; a world where we can say that the peace we enjoy in our hearts, in our families, in our communities and among nations is largely the outcome of love.

Building that peace is a common task. United we can do it.

(The Spiritual Forum of Santiago for Peace, 2003)

Described in the Chicago press in 1893 as "the greatest figure in the Parliament of Religions," Swami Vivekananda (1863–1901) and his spiritual master Sri Ramakrishna led Hinduism into the modern world. This text is excerpted from his opening address to the Parliament.

I will quote to you . . . a few lines from a hymn which I remember to have repeated from my earliest boyhood, which is every day repeated by millions of human beings: "As the different streams having their sources in different places all mingle their water in the sea, so, O Lord, the different paths which men take through different tendencies, various though they appear, crooked or straight, all lead to Thee.". . .

Sectarianism, bigotry, and its horrible descendant, fanaticism, have long possessed this beautiful earth. They have filled the earth with violence, drenched it often and often with human blood, destroyed civilization, and sent whole nations to despair. Had it not been for these horrible demons, human society would be far more advanced than it is now. But their time is come; and I fervently hope that the bell that tolled this morning in honour of this convention may be the death-knell of all fanaticism, of all persecutions with the sword or with the pen, and of all uncharitable feelings between persons wending their way to the same goal.

This selection by famed anthropologist Margaret Mead (1901–1978) is from her 1975 book World Enough. *Mead wrote 44 books and a thousand articles in her long career researching the lives of ordinary people throughout the world.*

What we need most are ways of thinking and acting through which we will not be overwhelmed by increasing scale, nor driven to despair or cruel indifference by the magnitudes with which we must deal. This is a central problem for us who are conscious and sentient beings, living in the midst of an evolutionary process with a beginning on this planet which we can only guess at and a future for which we must take responsibility without being able to know in what direction it may go.

The importance of each daily act—rising in the morning to the day's tasks, spending an hour explaining to a sick child in a hospital how a caterpillar turns into a butterfly, sending a few dollars to relieve famine in another part of the world—have to be brought into relationship with our decisions to build more and more missiles or to consign a million tons of grain to one country instead of another.

If we can see the Nigerian fishermen with their age-old nets, the Balinese farmer plowing his land for the planting of rice, and the hungry child in India, all as parts of a whole of which we are, not distant spectators, but a part; if we can see not only power-hungry manipulators, on the one hand, and oppressed and dying people, on the other, but both—and all—caught in the same moment in history, a moment when the whole future of life on the earth, and even possibly life in the galaxy, or the universe, is at stake, the very vastness of the process can ennoble the smallest hope, deflate the most grandiose dream of world dominion, and reduce species-wide guilt to human scale, making possible action by human beings on behalf of human beings.

Dr. Ntate Kgalushi Koka is director of the Karaites Institute of Afri-cology in South Africa. His description of the Ceremony of the Ashes was given to participants at the regional Southern Africa Inter-Faith Conference in Johannesburg under the theme "Promoting Peace and Harmony," October 2003.

Friends—African Traditional Religions believe in the universal con-cept of UBuntu (humanness) that recognizes the equality and in-herent spirituality of every human being. This humanness is instilled in our bodies through the divine spirit, converting them into living souls. We know that even our greatest enemy is our brother or sister. The being-ness of the other person is mirroring my own human-ness. This philosophical foundation is only a potentiality. It has to be actualized in practical ways to bring about peace in conflict sit-uations. Rituals and ceremonies are ways of doing this. Rituals make the spiritual forces visible in actions and gestures.

The Ceremony of the Ashes is an example of this. During the ritual, two persons or parties in conflict are gathered by community elders. The two adversaries have to face each other, while ash is placed in their hands. They then have to lick the ash from each other's hands and spit it out. The washing of hands, a handshake and embracing follow the action.

The ash is a symbol of something that has burned but whose energy has been spent. By licking up the ash and spitting it out, the quarrelling persons symbolically act out that the evil energy of their quarrel has been used up. This ceremony must take place within the community. Conflict isolates people from the community, while the healing ritual accepts people back into the group.

A scholar of the teachings of Confucius, Mencius (second century BCE) tried to lecture to rulers about good government following the Master's principles. In later life, Mencius wrote seven books about the ideals of benevolent governing. He believed all humans had an innate sense of right and wrong that could be used "to labor for the good of the common people."

The prince of Lu wanting to commit the administration of his government to the disciple Yo-ching, Mencius said, "When I heard of it, I was so glad that I could not sleep."

Gung sun Zhou asked, "Is Yo-ching a man of vigour?" and was

answered, "No." "Is he wise in council?" "No." "Is he possessed of much information?" "No."

"What then made you so glad that you could not sleep?"

"He is a man who loves what is good."

"Is the love of what is good sufficient?"

"The love of what is good is more than a sufficient qualification for the government of the empire; —how much more is it so for the state of Lu!"

(The Books of Mencius, VI)

In about 610 during one of his periodic meditative retreats in a cave near Mecca, the Prophet Muhammad (570–632 CE) began to experience visions and auditory revelations. An angel commanded him to reveal to his people messages from Allah. These were collected into the Qur'an, the most holy of Muslim scriptures, from which the following is an excerpt.

What actions are most excellent?
To gladden the heart of a human being.
To feed the hungry.

To help the afflicted.

To lighten the sorrow of the sorrowful.

To remove the wrongs of the injured.

That person is the most beloved of God who does most good to
God's creatures.

*This reading is taken from a sacred text of the sayings of the Buddha
(c. fifth century BCE), or Awakened One. Buddhism has been called
"The Light of Asia" and now has a vast influence on the diverse peoples of all continents.*

Worse is he who, when reviled, reviles again.

One, who, when reviled, doth not revile again

A two-fold victory wins.

He seeks the good both of the other and himself;

For, he the other's angry mood doth understand,

And groweth calm and still.

He is a physician of both,

Since he healeth himself and the other, too.

(Majjhima Nikaya Samyutta Nikaya, 7.1.2. and ll.1.4)

The sayings of the Chinese social philosopher K'ung Fu-Tzu, commonly known as Confucius (551–479 BCE), were collected after his death into a book entitled The Analects. His teachings, revered even today, emphasized education and correct behavior, not military might, for rulers and for families.

The disciple Zigong put a question relative to government. In reply the Master mentioned three essentials: sufficient food, sufficient armament, and the people's confidence.

"But," said the disciple, "if you cannot really have all three, and one has to be given up, which would you give up first?"

"The armament," he replied.

"And if you are obliged to give up one of the remaining two, which would it be?"

"The food," said he. "Death has been the portion of all men from of old. Without the people's trust nothing can stand. . . ."

The disciple Jikang, when consulting Confucius about the government, said, "Suppose I were to put to death the disorderly for the better encouragement of the orderly—what say you to that?"

"Sir," replied Confucius, "in the administration of government why resort to capital punishment? Covet what is good, and the people will be good. The virtue of the noble-minded man is as the wind, and that of inferior men as grass; the grass must bend, when the wind blows upon it."

These words were spoken by Dag Hammarskjold (1905–1961) as part of the dedication speech for the United Nations Prayer Room near the entrance to the UN Building in New York. Hammarskjold's term as Secretary-General of the UN, from 1953 to 1961, ended tragically when he died in an airplane crash in Africa. He was from Sweden.

We have reached a critical point in history, where we must turn to God to avoid the consequences of our own faulty thinking. We must pray, not a few of us, but all of us. We must pray simply, fervently, sincerely, and with increasing power as our faith grows. We must condition the world's leaders by asking God's Spirit to descend upon their hearts and minds. We must condition ourselves and each and every one by asking God's help in living so that peace may be possible.

We must pray in church, at home, on the train, while driving, on the job—and keep at it. Each of us is important now. The ability of every individual to seek divine help is a necessary link in the golden chain of harmony and peace.

Prayer is a dynamic manifestation of love by the concerned, reaching out for God's help. You can help change the world by your prayers and your prayerful action.

The Prophet Isaiah, one of the latter prophets in the Hebrew canon, is estimated to have lived from 742 to 701 BCE when the Northern Kingdom was conquered by the Assyrian empire. The prophets were passionate, extraordinary people who dared to voice their understanding of God's will for the future, identified as peace, justice, fertility, righteousness, and joy.

Ah, you who make iniquitous decrees,
who write oppressive statutes,
to turn aside the needy from justice
and to rob the poor of my people of their right,
that widows may be your spoil,
and that you may make the orphans your prey!
What will you do on the day of punishment,
in the calamity that will come from far away?

To whom will you flee for help,
and where will you leave your wealth,
so as not to crouch among the prisoners
or fall among the slain?

For all this God's anger has not turned away;
his hand is stretched out still.

> (Holy Bible, the Hebrew Scriptures, Isaiah 10:1–4)

The most widely known of all Buddhist scriptures, the Dhammapada (c. 240 BCE) is also one of the most ancient of sacred scriptures with some sayings in it attributed to the Buddha himself. Sometimes called "The Buddhist Gospel," it is in use by schoolchildren in many Buddhist countries even today. This selection is from a group of sayings entitled "Punishment" within the Dhammapada.

All men tremble at punishment, all men fear death; remember that thou art like unto them, and do not kill, nor cause slaughter.

All men tremble at punishment, all men love life; remember that thou art like unto them, and do not kill, nor cause slaughter.

He who, seeking his own happiness, punishes or kills beings who also long for happiness, will not find happiness after death.

A Buddhist monk from Vietnam, Thich Nhat Hanh leads seminars on mindfulness in many parts of the world and has written several books describing how people can live according to the highest religious values.

No single tradition monopolizes the truth. We must glean the best values of all traditions and work together to remove the tensions between traditions in order to give peace a chance. We need to join together and look deeply for ways to help people get rerooted.

We need to propose the best physical, mental, and spiritual health plan for our nation and for the earth. For a future to be possible, I urge you to study and practice the best values of your religious tradition and to share them with young people in ways they can understand. If we meditate together as a family, a community, a city, and a nation, we will be able to identify the causes of our suffering and find ways out.

(*Living Buddha, Living Christ*)

The Gemara, or "Learning," evolved over three centuries of discussions in rabbinical academies to interpret the even more ancient Mishnah, one of Judaism's sacred scriptures for regulating Jewish life. The Gemara, when combined with the Mishnah, is called the Talmud.

Rabbi Baruka of Huza frequented the market of Lapet. One day Elijah (the Prophet) appeared to him there, and Rabbi Baruka asked him: "Is there among the people of this market any one that is destined to share in the World to Come?" Elijah replied, "There is none." But then two men appeared on the scene, and Elijah said to Rabbi Baruka, "No, here are two who will share in the World to Come."

Rabbi Baruka then asked them, "What is your occupation?" They said, "We are merry-makers. When we see a man who is downcast, we cheer him up; also when we see two people quarreling, we endeavor to make peace between them."

(The Gemara, Ta'anit, 22a, c. 500 CE)

In this selection from the text entitled "The Shijing," Confucius (551–497 BCE) gives a warning to governors in China on how to behave toward their people. The text is an anthology of ancient hymns and poetic eulogies compiled by the Master.

God has reversed his usual course of procedure,
And the lower people are full of distress.
The words which you utter are not right;
The plans which you form are not far-reaching.
As there are not sages, you think you have no guidance; —
You have no real sincerity.
Thus your plans do not reach far,
And I therefore strongly admonish you.

Heaven is now sending down calamities; —
Do not be so complacent.
Heaven is now producing such movements; —
Do not be so indifferent.
If your words were harmonious,
The people would become united.

If your words were gentle and kind,
The people would be settled.

Attributed to Lao Tzu, the legendary founder of Taoism, the Tao Te Ching is called "The Classic of the Way and Virtue." This text, written in the fifth-to-second century BCE, has been translated more times and into more languages than any book in history except the Bible. The central teaching of the Tao, or "Way," is to live in harmony with it and find fulfillment in life.

Alive, a man is supple, soft;
In death, unbending, rigid.
All creatures, grass and trees, alive
Are plastic but are pliant too,
And dead, are withered and dry.
Unbending rigor is the concomitant of death,
And yielding softness, the concomitant of life:
Unbending soldiers get no victories;
The stiffest tree is ripe for the axe.

The strong and mighty topple from their place;
The soft and yielding rise above them all.

(Tao Te Ching, 76)

The two prayers that follow are based on ancient scriptures and can be used at the concluding service for Yom Kippur, the holiest of Jewish holidays.

Compassionate God, let the promise be fulfilled: "I will bring peace to the land; you shall be serene and unafraid. I will rid the land of vicious beasts, and the sword of war shall be set aside. They shall beat their swords into plowshares, and their spears into pruning-hooks; nation shall not lift up sword against nation, nor ever again shall they train for war. Justice shall roll down like waters, righteousness as a mighty stream."

Source of all being, we turn to You as did our people in ancient days. They beheld You in the heavens; they felt You in their hearts; they sought You in their lives.

Now their quest is ours. Help us, O God, to see the wonder of being. Give us the courage to search for truth. Teach us the path to a better life. So shall we, by our lives and our labors, bring nearer to realization the great hope inherited from ages past, for a world transformed by liberty, justice, and peace.

(Stern, ed., *Gates of Repentance*)

Vaclav Havel, former president of the Czech Republic, spoke these words at Independence Hall in Philadelphia in 1994. A playwright, politician, and eloquent human rights activist, Havel continues to speak out on world issues from a deeply moral perspective.

The only real hope of people today is probably a renewal of our certainty that we are rooted in the Earth and at the same time, the cosmos. This awareness endows us with the capacity for self-transcendence.

Politicians at international forums may reiterate a thousand times that the basis of the new world order must be universal respect for human rights, but it will mean nothing as long as this imperative does not derive from the respect of the miracle of Being, the miracle of the universe, the miracle of nature, the miracle of our own existence. Only someone who submits to the authority of the universal order and of creation, who values the right to be a part of it and a participant in it, can genuinely value himself and his neighbors and thus honor their rights as well.

It follows that, in today's multicultural world, the truly reliable path to peaceful coexistence and creative cooperation must start from what is at the root of all cultures and what lies infinitely deeper in human hearts and minds than political opinion, convictions, antipathies or sympathies: it must be rooted in self-transcendence.

The (U.S.) Declaration of Independence, adopted 218 years ago in this building, states that the Creator gave man the right to liberty. It seems man can realize that liberty only if he does not forget the One who endowed him with it.

Rowan Williams, Archbishop of Canterbury, wrote these words for the Times Literary Supplement *in 2003. They speak to the way religion can be involved in world events to bring greater hope to peoples suffering the consequences of political oppression.*

The oppressor needs the Abrahamic religions to be reminded of the imperatives for historical justice; while the heirs of the oppressed need a Buddhist discipline to free them from historical resentment. Two therapies for a truthful memory; these words have immense resonance just now.

These words of Jimmy Carter, the thirty-ninth president of the United States, are excerpted from his address accepting the Nobel Peace Prize in 2002 Carter has worked tirelessly for resolution of world conflicts during his retirement years.

I am not here as a public official, but as a citizen of a troubled world who finds hope in a growing consensus that the generally accepted goals of society are peace, freedom, human rights, environmental quality, the alleviation of suffering and the rule of law. During the past decades the international community, usually under the auspices of the United Nations, has struggled to negotiate global agreements that can help us achieve these essential goals.

They include the abolition of land mines and chemical weapons; an end to the testing, proliferation and further deployment of nuclear warheads; constraints on global warming; prohibition of the death penalty, at least for children; and an international criminal court to deter and to punish war crimes and genocide. . . .

War may sometimes be a necessary evil. But no matter how necessary, it is always evil, never a good. We will not learn how to live together in peace by killing each other's children.

The bond of our common humanity is stronger than the divisiveness of our fears and prejudices. God gives us a capacity for choice. We can choose to alleviate suffering. We can choose to work together for peace. We can make these changes—and we must.

An Australian, Dr. Helen Caldicott left clinical medicine to work full-time waking the world to the threat of nuclear annihilation. She co-founded the international group Physicians for Social Responsibility, is the author of five books, and was a faculty member at Harvard Medical School. Most recently she created the Nuclear Policy Research Institute as a public education center.

In 2003 the danger persists unbeknownst to the world. Russia and America still target each other with 2,500 hydrogen bombs on tenuous hair-trigger alert, and Russia's early-warning system is dangerously eroded. Regional nuclear conflict in North Korea, India or Pakistan could trigger global nuclear catastrophe. . . .

Nuclear weapons and nuclear energy are medically contraindicated for all life on earth. As a physician I consider it my responsibility to preserve and further life. Thus, as a doctor as well as a mother and a world citizen, I wish to practice the ultimate form of preventive medicine by ridding the earth of these technologies that propagate disease, suffering and death. . . .

It is vital that people be presented with the truth. . . . Today more than ever, we need what Einstein referred to as a "chain reaction of awareness."

Inventor, architect, engineer, mathematician, poet, and cosmologist, the American R. Buckminster Fuller (1895–1983) has been called the "Planet's Friendly Genius." He achieved worldwide fame as the inventor

of the geodesic dome, one of the strongest and least expensive forms of shelter. His prediction in 1970 that the planet could feed and clothe everyone on earth was confirmed by a 1977 World Food and Nutrition Study prepared by 1,500 scientists.

Think of it. We are blessed with technology that would be indescribable to our forefathers. We have the wherewithal, the know-it-all, to feed everybody, clothe everybody, give every human on earth a chance. We know now what we could never have known before—that we now have an option for all humanity to "make it" successfully on this planet in this lifetime. Whether it is to be Utopia or Oblivion will be a touch-and-go relay race right up to the final moment.

French philosopher and theologian Jacques Ellul (1912–1994) was a passionate critic of modern technology and what he believed was its threat to human freedom and religious faith.

Action really receives its character from prayer. Prayer is what attests the finitude of action and frees it from its dramatic or tragic aspect.

Since it shows that the action is not final, it brings to it humor and reserve. Otherwise we would be tempted to take it with dreadful seriousness. . . .

Prayer, because it is the warrant, the expression of my finitude, always teaches me that I must be more than my action, that I must live with my action and even that my action must be lived with by another in his action. Thanks to prayer, I can see that truth about myself and my action, in hope and not in despair.

(*Prayer and Modern Man*)

These words are from a sermon preached at Harvard's Memorial Church by Professor Paul Tillich (1886–1965), a renowned Christian theologian.

The goal of mankind is not progress toward a final stage of perfection; it is the creation of what is possible for us in each particular state of history; and it is the struggle against the forces of evil, old ones and new ones, which arise in each period in a different way.

There will be victories as well as defeats in these struggles. There will be progress and regressions. But every victory, every particular progress from injustice to more justice, from suffering to more happiness, from hostility to more peace, from separation to more unity anywhere in humankind, is a manifestation of the eternal in time and space. It is, in the language of the Old and the New Testaments, the coming of the Kingdom of God. For the Kingdom of God does not come in one dramatic event sometime in the future. It is coming here and now in every act of love, in every manifestation of truth, in every moment of joy, in every experience of the holy. . . .

The hope of humankind lies in the here and now, whenever the eternal appears in time and history. This hope is justified; for there is always a presence and a beginning of what is seriously hoped for.

(*Theology of Peace*)

There are 150 psalms in the Bible. These texts of hymns and prayers from the Jewish tradition were collected over centuries in the ancient past.

Let me hear the words of the Lord: are they not words of peace, peace to his people and his loyal servants and to all who turn and trust in him?

Deliverance is near to those who worship him, so that glory may dwell in our land.

Love and fidelity have come together; justice and peace join hands.

(Holy Bible, the Hebrew Scriptures, Psalm 85:8–10)

These words from the book of the Jewish prophet Isaiah in the Hebrew scriptures have been altered to fit a youth hymn-song of today. Isaiah, whose wife was also a prophet, was critical of both religious and political institutions.

Those who wait on the Lord
Shall renew their strength.
They shall rise up on wings as eagles.
They shall run and not be weary,
They shall walk and not faint.
Help us Lord, help us Lord, in Thy Way.

(Holy Bible, the Hebrew Scriptures, Isaiah 40:31)

Kofi Annan, the Secretary-General of the United Nations, was, like citizens of all nations, shocked by the tragic terrorist attacks on New York City's World Trade Center and other locations on September 11, 2001. Annan, who along with the UN received the Nobel Peace Prize that same year, offered these words about terrorism.

Terrorism threatens every society. As the world takes action against it, we have all been reminded of the need to address the conditions that permit the growth of such hatred and depravity. We must confront violence, bigotry and hatred even more resolutely. The United Nations' work must continue as we address the ills of conflict, ignorance, poverty and disease.

Doing so will not remove every source of hatred or prevent every act of violence. There are those who will hate and who will kill even if every injustice is ended. But if the world can show that it will carry on, that it will persevere in creating a stronger, more just, more benevolent and more genuine international community across all lines of religion and race, then terrorism will have failed.

French Emperor Napoleon I (Napoleon Bonaparte, 1769–1821) attempted to rule the European world of his time, including Russia, where he met one of his epic military defeats. He died in exile after causing millions of deaths in many countries.

There are only two powers in the world—the power of the sword and the power of the spirit. In the long run, the sword will always be conquered by the spirit.

The Golden Rule is found in one form or another in the ancient sacred texts of the major religions of the world, important precepts undergirding the hope for peace among all peoples.

HINDUISM: "This is the sum of duty: Do naught unto others which would cause you pain if done to you."

(Mahabharata 5, 1517)

BUDDHISM: "Hurt not others in ways that you yourself would find hurtful."

(Udana-Varga 5, 18)

CONFUCIANISM: "Is there one maxim which ought to be acted upon throughout one's whole life? Surely it is the maxim of lovingkindness. Do not unto others what you would not have them do unto you."

(Analects 15, 23)

TAOISM: "Regard your neighbor's gain as your own gain, and your neighbor's loss as your own loss."

(T'ai Shang Kan Ying P'ien)

ZOROASTRIANISM: "That nature alone is good which refrains from doing unto another whatsoever is not good for itself."

(Dadistan-i-dinik 94, 5)

JUDAISM: "What is hateful to you, do not to your fellowman. That is the entire Law; all the rest is commentary."

(Talmud, Shabbat 31a)

CHRISTIANITY: "All things whatsoever ye would that others should do to you, do ye even so to them: for this is the Law and the Prophets." (Holy Bible, the Christian Scriptures, Matthew 7:12)

ISLAM: "No one of you is a believer until he desires for his brother that which he desires for himself."

(Sunnah)

Published in 1930, these words from Mahatma Gandhi (1869–1948), considered by many to be the greatest moral leader of the twentieth century, were from a pamphlet distributed by the Fellowship of Reconciliation. He led the struggle for Home Rule from Britain in India, preaching nonviolent civil disobedience. He was assassinated by a religious zealot after India became independent.

The law of love will work, just as the law of gravitation will work, whether we accept it or not. Just as the scientist will work wonders out of various applications of the law of nature, even so a man who applies the law of love with scientific precision can work greater wonders. For the force of nonviolence is infinitely more wonderful and subtle than the material forces of nature, like, for instance, electricity.

Those who discovered for us the law of love were greater scientists than any of our modern scientists. Only our explorations have not gone far enough and so it is not possible for everyone to see all its workings. Such, at any rate, is the hallucination, if it is one, under which I am laboring. The more I work at this law the more I feel the delight in life, the delight in the scheme of this universe. It gives me a peace and a meaning of the mysteries of nature that I have no power to describe.

Famed Chinese composer of the score for the movie Crouching Tiger, Hidden Dragon, *Tan Dun has been awarded both a Grammy and an Oscar for his work. His* Water Passion after Saint Matthew *was commissioned to honor Bach's 250th birthday and premiered in Germany in 2001. In notes accompanying the recording of this work, Tan Dun comments on the rich and hopeful symbol of water.*

"So many cultures use water as an essential metaphor—there is the symbolism of baptism; it is associated with birth, creation, and re-creation. If you think of the water cycle, where it comes down to earth and returns to the atmosphere, only to return—that is a symbol of resurrection. I think of resurrection not only as a return to life but as a metaphor for hope, the birth of a new world, a better life."

Tan Dun's composition for orchestra and chorus entitled *Water Passion after Saint Matthew* begins and ends with the sound of water played by percussionists at seventeen transparent water bowls. They are lit from below and form a large cross that separates the playing areas for two mixed choruses and soloists. The percussionists use smooth-contoured stones, water gongs, water drums, paddles, water shakers, and Tibetan cymbals as well as fingers to create the water sounds. With them, the only other instruments used in the work are a *xun* (an ancient Chinese flute), a cello-like Chinese *erhu*, a Mongolian horse-head fiddle, a *kemanche* fiddle from the Middle East, and conventional Western cello and violin. Tan goes beyond the traditional telling of the Passion by beginning with Christ's baptism and ending with an evocation of resurrection, suggesting, in the words of the biblical book of Ecclesiastes sung by the choruses: ". . . a time to love, a time of Peace, a time to dance, a time of silence."

(Paraphrased from text in the Sony CD,
Water Passion after St. Matthew, 2001)

American artist Judy Chicago's unique artistic installation of ceramic and fabric place settings entitled The Dinner Party *(1979) was dedicated to famous women in world history. She is the author of the following visionary work entitled "Merger Poem."*

And then all that has divided us will merge
And then compassion will be wedded to power
And then softness will come to a world that is
harsh and unkind
And then both men and women will be gentle
And then both women and men will be strong
And then no person
will be subject to another's will
And then all will be rich and free and varied
And then the greed of some
will give way to the needs of many

And then all will share equally
in the earth's abundance
And then all will care
for the sick and the weak and the old
And then all will nourish the young
And then all will cherish life's creatures
And then all will live
in harmony with each other and the earth.
And then everywhere
will be called Eden once again.

(Ford-Grabowsky, ed., *Prayers for All People*)

The mystical vision of the biblical book of Revelation has inspired Christians for centuries to see hope for an end to suffering through the compassion of a beneficent God.

And I heard a loud voice from the throne saying:
"See the home of God is among mortals.
God will dwell with them, they shall be God's people,
and God indeed will be with them,

God will wipe every tear from their eyes,

Death will be no more;

mourning and crying and pain will be no more,

for the first things have passed away."

And the one who sat upon the throne said, "See, I am making all things new."

(Holy Bible, the Christian Scriptures, Revelation 21:3–5)

Lead Me from Hate to Love

The opposite of love is not hate but indifference—a lack of caring about what happens to a specific person, a suffering people, or, perhaps, to the future of humankind. A popular aphorism among the socially concerned says that the only thing necessary for evil to triumph is for the good to do nothing.

Apathy—a lack of active caring about anything—may be a barrier to peace greater than all the others. It creates a breeding ground for extremism, for inhumanity to flourish.

Bigotry—hatred for others—flourishes in societies where religious and political leaders ignore signs of it. An ancient word of wisdom from the Bible says "all is vanity"—another term for "pride" in the negative sense of believing one is superior to others. Races, cultures, and religions can also use bigotry to justify conflicts and wars and to demonize the other. All religions teach us not to follow that human tendency—we can choose the option of compassion for all of life, a stance requiring humility.

Compassion can lead to acts of love for ourselves and for others, restoring harmony in our families and societies.

This story from the teachings of the Buddha was among the first to be translated into English because it was held in such high esteem. It also was translated from the ancient Pali into Chinese as early as 67 CE.

And the Blessed One observed the ways of society and noticed how much misery came from malignity and foolish offences done only to gratify vanity and self-seeking pride.

And the Buddha said: "If a man foolishly does me wrong, I will return to him the protection of my ungrudging love; the more evil comes from him, the more good shall go from me; the fragrance of goodness always comes to me, and the harmful air of evil goes to him."

A foolish man, learning that the Buddha observed the principle of great love which commends the return of good for evil, came and abused him. The Buddha was silent, pitying his folly.

When the man had finished his abuse, the Buddha asked him, saying: "Son, if a man declined to accept a present made to him, to whom would it belong?" And he answered: "In that case, it would belong to the man who offered it."

"My son," said the Buddha, "thou hast railed at me but I decline to accept thy abuse, and request thee to keep it thyself. Will it not be a source of misery to thee? As the echo belongs to the sound, and the shadow to the substance, so misery will overtake the evildoer without fail."

The abuser made no reply, and the Buddha continued:

"A wicked man who reproaches a virtuous one is like one who looks up and spits at heaven; the spittle soils not the heaven, but comes back and defiles his own person.

"The slanderer is like one who flings dust at another when the wind is contrary; the dust does but return on him who threw it. The virtuous man cannot be hurt and the misery that the other would inflict comes back on himself."

The abuser went away ashamed, but he came again and took refuge in the Buddha, the Dharma (following the "law"), and the Sangha (community of converts).

(The Sutra in Forty-Two Sections, third century BCE)

One of the later monotheistic religions, Sikhism was founded by Guru Nanak in the fifteenth century CE in northern India, where most of its adherents live today. Its sacred scriptures are mainly hymns. Devotion to God and denial of selfish concerns are at the heart of the Sikh faith. Contrary customs are the topic of this thought from the Sikh writer Bhai Gurdas (c. 1553–1629).

The custom of the world is to return good for good;
    Of the spiritual teacher, good for evil.

(Vaar 28)

Saint Paul visited and corresponded with early followers of Christ throughout the Mediterranean, including those in Rome. His letters comprise much of the Bible's New Testament. The verses that follow are sometimes identified as the "Marks of the True Christian."

Let love be genuine; hate what is evil, hold fast to what is good;
  love one another with mutual affection; outdo one another in
  showing honor.
Do not lag in zeal, be ardent in spirit, serve the Lord.
Rejoice in hope, be patient in suffering, persevere in prayer.
Contribute to the needs of the saints;
  extend hospitality to strangers.
Bless those who persecute you; bless and
  do not curse them.
Rejoice with those who rejoice, weep with
  those who weep.
Live in harmony with one another; do not be haughty, but associate with the lowly;
  do not claim to be wiser than you are.
Do not repay anyone evil for evil, but take thought for what is
  noble in the sight of all.
If it is possible, so far as it depends on you, live peaceably
  with all.
          (Holy Bible, the Christian Scriptures, Romans 12:9–18)

His Holiness Tenzin Gyatso, the fourteenth Dalai Lama, is the exiled leader of Tibetan Buddhists. He now lives in a retreat center with many followers in Dharamsala, India. A winner of the Nobel Peace Prize in 1989, the Dalai Lama travels throughout the world teaching the central tenet of his faith, compassion for all life.

In the current world atmosphere, some people may think that religion is for those who remain in remote places and is not much needed in the areas of business or politics. My answer to this is "No!" For, as I have just said, in my simple religion, love is the key motivation. . . . Thus motivation is very important, and thus my simple religion is love, respect for others, honesty: teachings that cover not only religion but also the fields of politics, economics, business, science, law and medicine everywhere. With proper motivation these can help humanity; without it they go the other way. Without good motivation, science and technology, instead of helping, bring more fear and threaten global destruction. Compassionate thought is very important for humankind. . . .

It is helpful to have a variety of different approaches on the basis of a deep feeling of the basic sameness of humanity. We can then make joint effort to solve the problems of the whole of humankind. The problems human society is facing in terms of economic development, the crisis of energy, the tension between the poor and rich nations, and many geopolitical problems can be solved if we understand each other's fundamental humanity, respect each other's rights, share each other's problems and sufferings, and then make joint effort. . . .

Everybody loves to talk about calm and peace whether in a family, national, or international context, but without inner peace how can we make real peace? World peace through hatred and force is impossible. Even in the case of individuals, there is no possibility to feel happiness through anger. If in a difficult situation one becomes disturbed internally, overwhelmed by mental discomfort, then external things will not help at all. However, if despite external difficulties or problems, internally one's attitude is of love, warmth, and kindheartedness, then problems can be faced and accepted easily. . . .

Without love, human society is in a very difficult state; without love, in the future we will face tremendous problems. Love is the center of human life.

(Kindness, Clarity, and Insight)

The Testaments of the Twelve Patriarchs (second century BCE) are represented as a record of the dying declarations and instructions of the twelve sons of Jacob, later named Israel, a seminal figure in ancient Judaism.

Hatred is evil; it goes hand in hand with lying; it makes small things appear great; it leads to slander and stirs up war; it fills the heart with evil and poison. Thrust hatred from your heart; love one another from the heart. If someone commits a sin against you, speak peaceably to him; if he repents and confesses, forgive him. If a man is more successful than you, do not become vexed over it. Put envy out of your souls, and love one another with singleness of heart.

(quoted in Birnbaum, ed., *A Treasury of Judaism*)

Co-winner of the 1976 Nobel Peace Prize with her Protestant colleague Betty Williams, Máiread Corrigan-Maguire, a Catholic, tirelessly speaks out as a representative of the Peace People of Northern Ireland. This selection is from Corrigan-Maguire's address in 1999 to the International Peace Conference in Munich, Germany.

We can all do something for unity and peace.

We can each be generous, kind, forgiving and compassionate to ourselves, to everyone we meet and to the creation. We can, in a spirit of justice and unity, accept and celebrate the religious, sexual, cultural and political diversity of all men and women. We can honor the spirit of love living in our own heart and in the hearts of all our brothers and sisters, by refusing to harm or kill them.

We can, through the work of justice, create a better world for all, particularly the poor and the children, many of whom are suffering so much in the world today. We can each strive to live fully alive each moment in gratitude for the gift of life and creation.

The well-known mystical poet Jalal al-Din Rumi (1207–1273) of Persia was a major figure in early Sufism, the esoteric dimension of Islam, which continues to be recognized as a vital element in society. Rumi is credited with being responsible for assembling and contributing to The Masnavi, a collection of writings of deep spiritual import, from which the following excerpt is drawn.

Consider that visiting friends is a necessary custom, whatever they be, on foot, or mounted. And if it be an enemy, this act of kindness is still good, for many an enemy by kindness becomes a friend. And even if he does not become a friend, his enmity is lessened, since kindness is a salve to enmity. Besides these, there are many advantages in visiting, but I am fearful of prolixity, good friend. The sum and substance is this: be the friend of all. Like an idol-maker carve out a friend from stone because the multitude and concourse of a caravan will break the backs and the spears of highway robbers.

The Puranas are ancient collections of philosophy, stories, and laws from Hindu sacred scriptures still enjoyed by the public in modern India. The Bhagavata Purana (c. 200 CE) is the scripture of the life and teachings of Krishna, an embodiment of Vishnu, revered as the One God by Vaishnavite Hindus.

A dispute once arose among the sages which of the three gods was greatest. They applied to the greatest of all sages to determine the point. He undertook to put all three gods to a severe test.

He went first to Brahma, and omitted all obeisance. The god's anger blazed forth, but he was at length pacified.

Next he went to the abode of Siva, and omitted to return the god's salutation. The irascible god was enraged, his eyes flashed fire, and he raised his Trident weapon to destroy the sage. But the god's wife, Pirvatt, interceded for him.

Lastly, Bhrigu went to the heaven of Vishnu, whom he found asleep. To try his forbearance, he gave the god a good kick on his breast, which awoke him. Instead of showing anger, Vishnu asked Bhrigu's pardon for not having greeted him on the first arrival. Then he declared he was highly honored by the sage's blow. It had imprinted an indelible mark of good fortune on his breast. He trusted the sage's foot was not hurt, and began to rub it gently.

"This," said Bhrigu, "is the mightiest god; he overpowers his enemies by the most potent of all weapons—gentleness and generosity."

(Bhagavata Purana 10, 89)

Finding the source of this Native American tale "told many times around the Sacred Fire" is problematic, though many such authenticated

tales include a "grandfather" figure considered a substitute for the Great Spirit or God. It has been making the rounds of recent Internet sites without specific attribution, but it seems to represent an accepted view of some Native American wisdom traditions.

An old Grandfather said to his grandson, who came to him with anger at a friend who had done him an injustice. . . .

"Let me tell you a story. I too, at times, have felt great hate for those who have taken so much, with no sorrow for what they do. But hate wears you down, and does not hurt your enemy. It's like taking poison and wishing your enemy would die.

"I have struggled with these feelings many times.

"It is as if there are two wolves inside me; one is good and does no harm. He lives in harmony with all around him and does not take offense when no offense was intended. He will only fight when it is right to do so, and in the right way. But . . . the other wolf . . . ah! The littlest thing will send him into a fit of temper. He fights everyone, all of the time, for no reason. He cannot think because his anger and hate are so great. It is helpless anger, for his anger will change nothing.

"Sometimes it is hard to live with these two wolves inside me, for both of them try to dominate my spirit."

The boy looked intently into his Grandfather's eyes and asked, "Which one wins, Grandfather?"

The Grandfather smiled and quietly said, "The one I feed."

The Ramayana (fourth-to-third century BCE), a favorite text of Hindus even today, tells of the 1,001 adventures of Rama (later seen as an embodiment of the god Vishnu). Helped by the monkey god Hanuman, Rama succeeds in releasing his wife Sita from her abductor, the demon Ravana. Hanuman seeks to massacre the demon's supporters, but Sita says no—they were only obeying orders. She then quotes the following text.

You should not retaliate when another does you injury. Good conduct is the adornment of those who are good. Even if those who do wrong deserve to be killed, the noble ones should be compassionate, since there is no one who does not transgress.

Seneca (4 BCE–65 CE), a prominent citizen and playwright in ancient Rome, is quoted as saying hatred is "the most dangerous, outrageous, brutal, and intractable of all passions." A Stoic philosopher, Seneca believed in a Supreme Intelligence holding the universe in order and humans as having a "spark" of divine power within them.

Hatred is not only a vice, but a vice which goes point-blank
against Nature;
For it divides instead of joining, and frustrates the end of God's
will in human society.
One man was born to help another;
Hatred makes us destroy one another.
Love unites, hatred separates;
Love is beneficial, hatred is destructive.
Love succors even strangers, hatred destroys the most intimate
friendship;
Love fills all hearts with joy, hatred ruins all those who possess it.
Nature is bountiful, but hatred is pernicious;
For it is not hatred, but mutual love, that holds humankind together.

An English Benedictine monk, Bede Griffiths (1906–1994) lived in a Hindu ashram for much of his life and became a sannyasi *(an itinerant holy man). He studied the world's religions and shortly before his death completed a book, from which this selection was taken, on the unity of the world's religions.*

In every religion there are rituals and doctrines by which the Spirit makes itself known, but we have always to go beyond all rituals and doctrines to the Reality which they represent.

We cannot do without the rituals and doctrines, but if we remain at that level we become idolaters, not discerning the truth. So the Spirit in all religion is the Reality, which gives meaning to all observances. But there is one expression of the Spirit which is more meaningful than all others and that is love.

Love is invisible, but it is the most powerful force in human nature. Jesus spoke of the Spirit which he would send as Truth but also as Love. "If anyone loves me, my Father will love him and we will come to him and make our abode with him." This is the love, the prema and bhakti, which was proclaimed in the Bhagavad Gita, the compassion (karuna) of Buddha, the rapturous love of the Sufi saints.

Ultimately a religion is tested by its capacity to awaken love in its followers, and, what is perhaps more difficult, to extend that love to all humanity. In the past religions have tended to confine their love to their own followers, but always there has been a movement to break through these barriers and attain to a universal love.

(Universal Wisdom)

Muhyi al-Din ibn 'Arabi (1165–1240 CE) is described as one of Sufism's greatest teachers. He was born in Andalusia, Spain, and was a poet and traveler, writing many essays and books. He taught the "unity of being": All that really exists is utterly ineffable and we are God's attributes.

My heart has opened unto every form: it is a pasture for gazelles, a cloister for Christian monks, a temple for idols, the Ka'ba of the pilgrim, the tablets of the Torah and the book of the Qur'an. I practice the religion of Love. . . .

The biblical figure Jacob, who was later called Israel after his struggle with an angel, had twelve sons, including Gad. The Testament of Gad is from The Testaments of the Twelve Patriarchs, an ancient Jewish text (second century BCE) translated from the Hebrew and Aramaic, and includes this declaration.

Love ye one another from the heart; and if a man sin against thee, speak peaceably to him, and in thy soul hold not guile; and if he repent and confess, forgive him. But if he deny it, do not get into a passion with him, lest catching the poison from thee he take to swearing and so thou sin doubly.

Let not another man hear thy secrets when engaged in legal strife, lest he come to hate thee and become thy enemy, and commit a great sin against thee; for ofttimes he addresseth thee guilefully or burieth himself about thee with wicked intent. And though he deny it and yet have a sense of shame when reproved, give over reproving him. For he who denieth may repent so as not to wrong thee again; yea, he may also honor thee, and fear and be at peace with thee. But if he be shameless and persisteth in his wrong-doing, even so forgive him from the heart, and leave to God the avenging.

Theravada Buddhists refer to King Asoka's Edicts (304–232 BCE) as "The First Bill of Human and Animal Rights." The sayings were found inscribed in local languages on rock pillars in India, Pakistan, Nepal, and Afghanistan and are seen as historical evidence of a legal recognition of religious and cultural pluralism.

Wherein does religion consist? It consists in doing as little harm as possible, in doing good in abundance, in the practice of love, of compassion, of truthfulness and purity, in all the walks of life.

Among his many honors, Elie Wiesel has received the Nobel Peace Prize for his untiring efforts to promote goodwill among all people and to teach about the evils of hatred. A Holocaust survivor who was born in Romania, he lost his parents in Nazi concentration camps when he was sixteen years old. In his memoirs, he reflects on the nature of hate.

Hate—racial, tribal, religious, ancestral, national, social, ethical, political, economic, ideological—in itself represents the inexorable defeat of mankind, its absolute defeat. If there is an area in which mankind cannot claim the slightest progress, this surely is it. It does not take much for human beings, collectively or individually, to suddenly one day pit themselves like wild beasts one against the other, their worst instincts laid bare, in a state of deleterious exaltation. One decision, one simple word, and a family or a community will drown in blood or perish in flames.

Why is there so much violence, so much hate? How is it conceived, transmitted, fertilized, nurtured? As we face the disquieting, implacable rise of intolerance and fanaticism on more than one continent, it is our duty to expose the danger. By naming it. By confronting it.

(And the Sea Is Never Full)

Sometimes called "Verses of Righteousness," The Dhammapada (c. 240 BCE) contains pithy sayings on Buddhist practice and ethics. It is often used as a basic text for schoolchildren in Theravada Buddhist countries.

Anger must be overcome by the absence of anger;
Evil must be overcome by good;
Greed must be overcome by liberality;
Lies must be overcome by truth.

The Talmud includes The Torah and is the primary and most ancient sacred text for Jews today. Its readings on Jewish life and beliefs were compiled over centuries and codified around 350 CE.

When man appears before the Throne of Judgment, the first question he is asked is not, "Have you believed in God," or "Have you prayed and performed ritual acts," but "Have you dealt honorably, faithfully in all your dealings with your fellowman?"

(Talmud, Shabbat 31a)

The sacred writings of the Tao Te Ching (sixth century BCE) are attributed to the legendary founder of Taoism in China, Lao Tzu. He

taught about the mystical "Tao," or way of being that brings an individual closer to one's origin in nature. Taoism and Confucianism embrace the ancient Chinese belief that life requires a balance of forces—for example, Yin and Yang, good and evil, earth and heaven, male and female.

I have three treasures, which I hold and keep safe:
The first is called love; the second is called moderation;
The third is called not venturing to go ahead of the world.
Being loving, one can be brave; being moderate,
    one can be ample;
Not venturing to go ahead of the world,
    one can be the chief of all officials.
Instead of love, one has only bravery;
    instead of moderation, one has only amplitude;
Instead of keeping behind, one goes ahead:
Those lead to nothing but death.
For he who fights with love will win the battle; he who defends
    with love will be secure.
Heaven will save him, and protect him with love.

(Tao Te Ching 67)

Abdullah Ansari was a companion of the Prophet Muhammad (c. 570–632), who was the Messenger of Allah and the recipient of the words of the Qur'an, Islam's most holy scripture.

The law of life requires: sincerity to God, severity to self, justice to all people, service to elders.
Kindness to the young, generosity to the poor.
Good counsel to friends.
Forbearance with enemies.
Indifference to fools.
Respect to the learned.

The longest epic poem in world literature, the Mahabharata tells the Hindu story of a civil war between two clans and extols the virtues of courage, devotion to duty, and right living. The best-known section of the poem is the Bhagavad Gita, in which Krishna reveals his divinity to Arjuna, a warrior who questions the war.

They to whom good conduct is always dear,
 They who practice self-restraint,
They who have truth for their refuge, they who have mercy,
 They who are always ready to work for others,
They who are universal benefactors,
 They who are endowed with great courage,
They who follow all the duties sanctioned by the Scriptures,
 They who are devoted to the well-being of all,
They who give all, and sacrifice their very lives for others
 Are considered as good and virtuous.

(Mahabharata 12.158.23.24.25)

These instructions to his son are from one of the four Rightly Guided Caliphs recognized after the death of the Prophet Muhammad (c. 570–632). Ali Ibn-abi Talib was husband of the Prophet's daughter Fatima. He was regarded as a great scholar of Arabic literature.

My son, fear God both secretly and openly; speak the truth, whether you be calm or angry; be economical, whether you be poor or rich; be just to friend and foe; be resigned alike in times of adversity and prosperity. My son, he who sees his own faults has no time to see the faults of others; he who is satisfied with the allotments of Providence does not regret the past; he who unsheathes the sword of aggression will be killed by it; he who digs a pit for his brother will fall into it; he who takes to evil ways will be despised; he who commits excesses will be known to do them; he who associates with the base will be subject to constant suspicion; he who remembers death will be content with little in this world; he who boasts of his sins before men, God will bring him to shame.

Jainism was founded by Mahavira (the Jina, 599–527 BCE), who lived in India. Its oldest sacred text is the Acaranga Sutra, which contains laws for monks and nuns and a biography of the Jina. It supports a central Jain tenet of nonviolence toward all life forms.

All breathing, existing, living, sentient creatures should not be slain,
    nor treated with violence, nor abused,
    nor tormented, nor driven away.
This is the pure, unchangeable, eternal law.

(Acaranga Sutra I.4.1)

Chuang-tzu (fourth century BCE) is credited with organizing Taoism into a religious body. He was the first in a long line of religious leaders with political influence in early China. The writings attributed to him are known collectively as, simply, The Chuang-tzu. Taoism promotes the understanding of eternal harmony—Yin and Yang—a balance of life forces accessible through meditation.

By the warmth of affection they (good warriors) sought the harmony of joy, and to blend together all within the four seas.
And their wish was to plant this everywhere
as the chief thing to be pursued.
They endured insult without feeling it a disgrace.
They sought to save the people from fighting.
To save their age from war, they forbade aggression,
and sought to hush the weapons of strife.
In this way they went everywhere,
counseling the high and instructing the low.
Though the world might not receive them,
they only insisted on their object the more strongly.

(The Chuang-tzu 33.3)

A Chinese sage living between the years of Confucius and Mencius, Mo-tzu (second century BCE) rejected the secularism they taught and became a believer in heavenly spirits and earthly saints preaching love, truth, and goodness as absolutes. He thought the values of a patriarchal society inevitably led to war, and he became a pacifist.

Mo-tzu said: The purpose of the magnanimous is to be found in procuring benefits for the world and eliminating its calamities.

But what are the benefits of the world and what its calamities?

Mo-tzu said: Mutual attacks among states, mutual usurpation among houses, mutual injuries among individuals; the lack of grace and loyalty between ruler and ruled, the lack of harmony between elder and younger brothers—these are the major calamities in the world.

But whence did these calamities arise, out of mutual love?

Mo-tzu said: They arise out of want of mutual love. At present feudal lords have learned only to love their own states and not those of others. Therefore they do not scruple about attacking other states. The heads of houses have learned only to love their own houses and not those of others. Therefore they do not scruple about usurping other houses. And individuals have learned only to love themselves and not others. Therefore they do not scruple about injuring others. When feudal lords do not love one another there will be war on the fields. When heads of houses do not love one another they will usurp one another's power. When individuals do not love one another they will not be gracious and loyal. When father and son do not love each other they will not be affectionate and filial. When elder and younger brothers do not love each other they will not be harmonious. When nobody in the world loves any other, naturally the strong will overpower the weak, the many will oppress the few, the wealthy will mock the poor, the honoured will disdain the humble, the cunning will deceive the simple. Therefore all the calamities, strifes, complaints, and hatred in the world have arisen out of want of mutual love. Therefore the benevolent disapproved of this want.

Now that there is disapproval, how can we have the condition altered?

Mo-tzu said: It is to be altered by the way of universal love and mutual aid. . . .

But the gentlemen of the world would say: "So far so good. It is of course very excellent when love becomes universal. But it is only a difficult and distant ideal."

Mo-tzu said: This is simply because the gentlemen of the world do not recognize what is to the benefit of the world, or understand what is its calamity. Now, to besiege a city, to fight in the fields, or to achieve a name at the cost of death—these are what men find difficult. Yet when the superior encourages them, the multitude can do them. Besides, universal love and mutual aid is quite different from these. Whoever loves others is loved by others; whoever benefits others is benefited by others; whoever hates others is hated by others; whoever injures others is injured by others. Then, what difficulty is there with universal love? Only, the ruler fails to embody it in his government and the ordinary man in his conduct.

Jesus of Nazareth was a devout Jew and is also the central figure of the Christian religion. He is worshiped as the Incarnation of the one God, described as Father, Son, and Holy Spirit. He taught primarily through parables, in the rabbinical tradition, and often quoted from sacred scriptures. This famous parable is known as "The Good Samaritan."

And behold, a certain lawyer stood up and tempted him, saying, Master, what shall I do to inherit eternal life? He said unto him,

What is written in the law? how readest thou? And he answering said, Thou shalt love the Lord thy God with all thy heart, and with all thy strength, and with all thy mind; and thy neighbor as thyself. And he said unto him, Thou hast answered right; this do, and thou shalt live.

But he, willing to justify himself, said unto Jesus, And who is my neighbor? And Jesus answering said, A certain man went down from Jerusalem to Jericho, and fell among thieves, which stripped him of his raiment, and wounded him, and departed, leaving him half dead.

And by chance there came down a certain priest that way; and when he saw him, he passed by on the other side. And likewise a Levite [lay associate to priests], when he was at the place came and looked at him, and passed by on the other side. But a certain Samaritan [a foreigner] as he journeyed, came near where he was; and when he saw him, he had compassion on him, and went to him, and bound up his wounds, pouring in oil and wine, and set him on his own beast, and brought him to an inn, and took care of him.

Then on the morrow when he departed, he took out two pence, and gave them to the host, and said unto him, Take care of him; and whatever thou spendest more, when I come again, I will repay thee.

Which now of these three, thinkest thou, was neighbor to him who fell among the thieves?

And he said, He that shewed mercy on him.
Then said Jesus unto him, Go, and do thou likewise.
(Holy Bible, the Christian Scriptures, Luke 10:25–37)

The Mahabharata tells the story of an endless civil war between rival clans. On one side the leaders are evil and on the other good, but their warriors have family members in both clans. In a renowned section of the poem, the Bhagavad Gita, one of the good leaders turns out to be Krishna, an embodiment of the One God Vishnu according to Vaishnava Hindus.

To injure none by thought or word or deed,
To give to others, and be kind to all—
This is the constant duty of the good.
High-minded men delight in doing good,
Without a thought of their own interest;
When they confer a benefit on others,
They reckon not on favours in return.

(Mahabharata 3)

Those men succeed in ascending to heaven
 Who, meeting with friends or foes,
 Behave in the same friendly way towards all.

(Mahabharata 13)

The Tao Te Ching is the "Classic of the Way and Virtue" and is considered a collection of the teachings of Lao Tzu (fifth century BCE), founder of Taoism in China. Taoist sages teach a mystical union with the great pattern of nature, the impersonal Tao, through meditation and trance.

The highest goodness is like water. Water is beneficent to all things but does not contend. It stays in places which others despise. Therefore it is near Tao.
 In dwelling, think it a good place to live;
 In feeling, make the heart deep;
 In friendship, keep on good terms with men;
 In words, have confidence;
 In ruling, abide by good order;
 In business, take things easy;

In motion, make use of the opportunity.
Since there is no contention, there is no blame.

(Tao Te Ching 8)

Among the most influential leaders for peace in human history, Mahatma Gandhi (1869–1948) embodied sacrificial living and nonviolence as a means to achieve justice for oppressed peoples. Born to a Hindu family in India, he was raised in South Africa and India. He founded a worldwide movement for human rights that also inspired Martin Luther King Jr.'s dream for a nonracist America.

Man and his deed are two distinct things. It is quite proper to resist and attack a system, but to resist and attack its author is tantamount to resisting and attacking oneself. For we are all tarred with the same brush, and are children of one and the same Creator, and as such the divine powers within us are infinite. To slight a single human being is to slight those divine powers, and thus to harm not only that being but with him the whole world.

The Qur'an contains the recitations of the Prophet Muhammad (c. 570–632) as revealed to him by Allah. It is the most sacred scripture in all Islam.

[Saith the Lord:] "We have ordained that he who slayeth
any one,
  unless it be a person guilty of manslaughter
   or of spreading disorders in the land,
shall be as though he had slain all mankind;
  but that he who saveth a life
   shall be as though he had saved all mankind alive."

              (Qur'an 5:18)

The great Persian poet Jalal al-Din Rumi is considered the author of The Masnavi and many other treasured writings in Islamic literature. Rumi was a Sufi, from the mystical branch of Islam, which taught the universality of revelation and the unity of the inner message of religions. This excerpt from The Masnavi, titled "The Contention as to

Grapes of Four Persons, Each of Whom Knows Grapes by a Different Name," explores the confusions that can lead to unnecessary conflict.

A man gave a diram to four persons. One of them, a Persian, said, "I will spend this on 'angur.'"

Another of them was an Arab; he said, "No, you rogue; I want 'inab,' not 'angur.'"

A third was a Turk; he said, "I do not want 'inab,' dear friend, I want 'uzum.'"

The fourth was a Greek; he said, "Stop this altercation; I wish for 'istafil.'"

Those persons began to fight against one another, because they were ignorant of the secret of the names. Through sheer ignorance they struck one another with their fists; they were full of ignorance and devoid of knowledge.

If one who knew the inner truth, an estimable man versed in many tongues, had been there, he would have reconciled them. He would have said, "With this one diram I will gratify the desire of all of you. If in all sincerity you entrust your hearts to me, this diram of yours will do so much for you. Your one diram will become as four, which is what is wanted; four enemies will become as one by concord."

Although your words appear uniform and in harmony, they are the source, in their effect, of contention and anger.

The earliest of all Jain texts, the Acaranga Sutra was preserved in the language of Prakrit spoken by the founder Mahavira. He spent twelve years as an ascetic before entering enlightenment and reaching complete omniscience as "The Perfected One." The Jain renunciation of killing is expressed in this piece from the Acaranga Sutra.

All beings are fond of life; they like pleasure and hate pain, shun destruction and like to live, they long to live. To all, life is dear.

Living beings should not be slain, nor treated with violence, nor abused, nor tormented, nor driven away. . . .

I renounce all killing of living beings, whether subtle or gross, whether movable or immovable. Nor shall I myself kill living beings nor cause others to do it, nor consent to it.

He who injures does not comprehend and renounce the sinful acts; he who does not injure comprehends and renounces the sinful acts. Knowing them, a wise man should not act sinfully towards animals, nor cause others to act so, nor allow others to do so.

The Tevigga Sutta is part of a long argument by the Buddha (c. fifth century BCE) against the teachings of the priests of Brahminism in India over why they cannot guide people to union with the Infinite. This can be achieved only through "right conduct," he stressed, not the rituals the priests so rigorously practiced.

The Blessed One was asked how one's conduct can be good.

"Putting away all judgment of others, he abstains from slander. What he hears he repeats not elsewhere to raise a quarrel; what he hears elsewhere he repeats not here to raise a quarrel. Thus he brings together those who are divided, he encourages those who are friendly; he is a peacemaker, a lover of peace, impassioned for peace, a speaker of words that make for peace. Putting away all bitter thoughts, he abstains from harsh language. Whatever is humane, pleasant to the ear, kindly, reaching to the heart, urbane, acceptable to the people, appreciated by the people—such are the words he speaks. . . . He abstains from all bribery, killing or maiming, abducting, highway robbery, plundering villages, or obtaining money by threats of violence. These are the kinds of goodness he practices."

An important successor to the Chinese master teacher Confucius, the philosopher known as Mencius wrote a book stressing the essential good-ness of human nature. He was a champion of the weak and called for rulers to improve the lives of ordinary people.

All men have a mind
    which cannot bear to see the sufferings of others.
If men suddenly see a child about to fall into a well,
    they will experience a feeling of alarm and distress.
Let them have their complete development,
    and they will suffice to love
        and protect all within the four seas.

                                (The Books of Mencius)

The definitive guide for all Muslims to live a life of devotion to Allah, the Qur'an ("The Recitation") was transmitted by an angel to the Prophet Muhammad during years of meditation in both Mecca and Medina, Arabia. It is divided into 114 chapters called surahs. Surah

107, here in its entirety, uses just a few words to emphasize the importance of taking care of those in need.

In the Name of the Most Merciful God: What thinkest thou of him who denieth the future judgment as a falsehood? It is he who pusheth away the orphan; and stirreth not up others to feed the poor. Woe be unto those who pray, and who are negligent at their prayer: who play the hypocrites, and deny necessaries to the needy.

A famous Jewish intellectual from Andalusia, Spain, Moses Maimonides (c. 1135–1204 CE) eventually settled in Cairo as a court physician. He is best known for his book The Guide for the Perplexed. *In this selection Maimonides addresses issues related to justice and compassion.*

Love truth and justice; hate falsehood and injustice. Stand behind your promises: let them be as binding as a written contract. Disdain mental reservation, trickery and evasion. Live honestly, conscientiously and cleanly. Let your loyalty to truth be your priceless wealth, for there is no heritage equal to honor.

Be compassionate to the poor and the sorrowing: let them share in your joys and attend your feasts. Avoid those who love friction. If your own relatives like to stir up strife, act like a stranger to them. Avoid revenge, for it may come back on your own head. Revenge results only in hatred, confusion and sleeplessness.

(Quoted in Birnbaum, *A Treasury of Judaism*)

The most ancient of all religious literature, the four collections of the Vedas are widely believed to have been gathered over a thousand years (from approximately 1400–400 BCE) out of the oral tradition in the Indus Valley of northern India. They consist of hymns, sacrificial rituals, and instructions to the faithful.

O God, scatterer of ignorance and darkness,
    grant me your strength.
May all beings regard me with the eye of a friend,
    and I all beings!
With the eye of a friend may each single being
    regard all others!

(Yojht Veda, xxxvi, 18)

This reading from the Buddhist text the Sutta Nipata (fifth century BCE) is called the Metta Sutta, which is often translated "The Buddha's Words on Kindness." It is considered one of the core teachings of Buddhism. The four divine conditions of the mind in Buddhism are compassion, loving-kindness, sympathetic joy, and equanimity.

This is what should be done
By one who is skilled in goodness,
And who knows the path of peace: . . .

Let none deceive another,
Or despise any being in any state.
Let none through anger or ill-will
Wish harm upon another.
Even as a mother protects with her life
Her child, her only child,
So with a boundless heart
Should one cherish all living beings:
Radiating kindness over the entire world
Spreading upwards to the skies,
And downwards to the depths;

Outwards and unbounded,
Freed from hatred and ill-will.
Whether standing or walking, seated or lying down
Free from drowsiness,
One should sustain this recollection.
This is said to be the sublime abiding.
By not holding to fixed views,
The pure-hearted one, having clarity of vision,
Being freed from all sense desires,
Is not born again into this world.

(Sutta Nipata, 145)

Corey Kilgannon is a reporter for the New York Times. *The following is a summary of an article by Kilgannon that appeared January 14, 2004 under the headline "Fighting Hate, Across Cultures and Generations."*

A young Christian survivor of the massacres of her people in Rwanda in 1994 and an elderly Jewish survivor of the Holocaust in Poland during World War II tell their stories to youth in America "to save other families from potential genocide" and to help heal their own pain. Both survivors, David Gewirtzman and Jacqueline Murekatete, lost their families in these horrific historical events.

Gewirtzman told a reporter: "We both went through a traumatic experience, but instead of remaining bitter and angry and seeking revenge, we both resolved to spend the anger in a positive manner, to prevent this from ever happening again."

Ms. Murekatete shows listeners that racial hatred has outlived the Holocaust, and that genocide was not just something that happened to an old Jewish man from Poland, Gewirtzman said.

"When I go to an inner-city school, the kids might think they have nothing in common with some Jews 60 years ago, or me with slavery," he said. "But when they see both of us, they see the problem is the same," he said. "It transcends race and ethnicity. People are still being taught hatred and it is hatred that we are fighting."

Ms. Murekatete said, "Sometimes, students ask if they can help, and I say, The best thing you can do for me is to educate yourselves so this doesn't continue to happen."

In the King James translation of the Bible, the word charity *is used where most contemporary translations choose the word* love *(with the understanding that it means "spiritual love"). This selection is from the first letter of Saint Paul to the fledging Christian community in Corinth, Greece. The text is considered one of the noblest in all of sacred literature.*

Though I speak with the tongues of men and of angels, and have not charity, I am become as sounding brass, or a tinkling cymbal. And though I have the gift of prophecy, and understand all mysteries, and all knowledge; and though I have all faith, so that I could remove mountains, and have not charity, I am nothing. And though I bestow all my goods to feed the poor, and though I give my body to be burned, and have not charity, it profiteth me nothing.

Charity suffereth long, and is kind, charity envieth not; charity vaunteth not itself, is not puffed up, doth not behave itself unseemly, seeketh not her own, is not easily provoked, thinketh no evil; rejoiceth not in iniquity, but rejoiceth in the truth; beareth all things, believeth all things, hopeth all things, endureth all things.

Charity never faileth: but whether there be prophecies, they shall fail; whether there be tongues, they shall cease; whether there be knowledge, it shall vanish away. For we know in part, and we prophesy in part. But when that which is perfect is come, then that which is in part shall be done away.

When I was a child, I spake as a child, I understood as a child, I thought as a child: but when I became a man, I put away childish things. For now we see through a glass, darkly; but then face to face: now I know in part; but then shall I know even as also I am known. And now abideth faith, hope, charity, these three; but the greatest of these is charity.

(Holy Bible, the Christian Scriptures, 1 Corinthians 13:1–13)

Lead Me from War to Peace

*A*ncient religious notions of peace for believers ranged from emptying one's mind of human passions (at peace within oneself) to peace as the absence of war.

In our time, understandings of peace are most often related to justice and human rights. We believe there can be no real peace until there is justice for all, until the common good is as important as personal well-being. However, this concept means wars and conflicts can be seen as a righteous, even religiously endorsed, means for achieving liberation from genocidal oppressions or injustices. In the wars in Kosovo and Iraq and the conflict between Palestinians and Israelis, all sides justify their violent actions on the basis of self-preservation. The ongoing "war on terror" is especially fearsome with its potential to inflict unbelievable destruction upon innocent civilians in the name of a justice coated with religious extremism. More traditional wars of conquest for greater power and land also continue to motivate greedy and proud rulers on several continents, some using children as their warriors.

Today nations cannot remain isolated from the vast currents of globalization that include its conflicts and injustices. Still, if war is to be prevented and peace is to prevail, the global task from religious perspectives is twofold: to become more loving persons and to promote the common good—worldwide. Fortunately there are compassionate global leaders and devout followers of core teachings in all religions who are working together to further both peace and justice.

Some of these ideas are eloquently presented in the readings that follow, inspiration for lighting a pathway to peace.

Taoism teaches that the way to a good society is not through educating people to fit into a society, but to enable each person to arrive at a state closer to nature by following the mystical Tao, or true way of life. Taoism's most sacred scripture, the Tao Te Ching (sixth century BCE),

*is attributed to its legendary founder, Lao Tzu, a philosopher-teacher in
ancient China.*

Disastrous years inevitably follow in the wake of
    great armies.

(Tao Te Ching 30.2)

Arms, however excellent, are unblest implements,
    detestable to all beings.
Therefore he who possesses the Tao, does not
    abide them.

(Tao Te Ching 31.1)

Peace and quietude are esteemed by the wise man;
    and even when victorious, he does not rejoice.
The killing of men fills multitudes with sorrow.
    We lament with tears because of it.

(Tao Te Ching 31.2.4)

The good commander is not imperious.
    The good fighter is not wrathful.
The greatest conqueror does not wage war.
    The best master governs by condescension.

This is the virtue of not contending.
   This is the virtue of persuasion.
This is the imitation of Heaven.
   And this was the highest aim of the ancients.

(Tao Te Ching 68.1.2)

A remarkable poet, writer, teacher, and devout Buddhist monk, Thich Nhat Hanh was exiled from his native Vietnam for promoting reconciliation between North and South Vietnam. Today he lives in southwestern France and travels the world teaching about the compassion at the heart of his faith. This poem, "Condemnation," considers the ways we understand the identity of our "enemy."

Listen to this:
yesterday six Vietcong came through my village,
and because of this, my village was bombed.
Every soul was killed.
When I returned to the village now, the next day,
there was nothing but clouds of dust—
the pagoda without roof or altar,

only the foundations of houses,
the bamboo thickets burned away.

Here in the presence of the undisturbed stars,
in the invisible presence of all people still alive on Earth,
let me raise my voice to denounce this dreadful war,
this murder of brothers by brothers!

Whoever is listening, be my witness:
I cannot accept this war.
I never could, I never will.
I must say this a thousand times before I am killed.

I am like the bird who dies for the sake of its mate,
dripping blood from its broken beak and crying out,
"Beware! Turn around and face your real enemies—
ambition, violence, hatred, and greed."

Humans are not our enemies—even those called "Vietcong."
If we kill our brothers and sisters, what will we have left?
With whom then shall we live?

(*Call Me By My True Names*)

Franklin D. Roosevelt (1882–1945) was president of the United States during World War II. His activist wife, Eleanor Roosevelt, became the first U.S. delegate to the United Nations and helped draft the Universal Declaration of Human Rights.

I have seen war. I have seen war on land and sea. I have seen blood running from the wounded. I have seen men coughing out their gassed lungs. I have seen the dead in the mud. I have seen cities destroyed.

I have seen 200 limping, exhausted men come out of the line—the survivors of a regiment of a thousand that went forward 48 hours before. I have seen children starving. I have seen the agony of mothers and wives. I hate war.

A preacher of Love, Truth, and Goodness for all creatures, Mo-tzu (second century BCE) was a pacifist during a warring period in Chinese history. It was said of him that he would "wear his head and heels off to help mankind."

The murder of one person is called unrighteous and incurs the death penalty. Following this argument, the murder of ten persons will be ten times as unrighteous and there should be ten death penalties; the murder of a hundred persons will be a hundred times as unrighteous and there should be a hundred death penalties.

All the gentlemen of the world know that they should condemn these things, calling them unrighteous. But when it comes to the great unrighteousness of attacking states, they do not know that they should condemn it. On the contrary, they applaud it, calling it righteous. And they are really ignorant of its being unrighteous. Hence they have recorded their judgment to bequeath to their posterity. If they did know that it is unrighteous, then why would they record their false judgment to bequeath to posterity? . . .

Now, about a country going to war. If it is winter it will be too cold; if it is summer it will be too hot. So it should be neither in winter nor in summer. If it is in spring it will take people away from sowing and planting; if it is in autumn it will take people away from reaping and harvesting. Should they be taken away in either of these seasons, innumerable people would die of hunger and cold.

And, when the army sets out, the bamboo arrows, the feather flags, the house tents, the armour, the shields, the sword hilts—innumerable quantities of these will break and rot and never come back. The spears, the lances, the swords, the poniards, the chariots, the carts—innumerable quantities of these will break and rot and never come back. Then innumerable horses and oxen will start out fat and come back lean or will not return at all. And innumerable people will die because their food will be cut off and cannot be supplied on account of the great distances of the roads. And innumerable people will be sick and die of the constant danger and the irregularity of eating and drinking and the extremes of hunger and over-eating. Then, the army will be lost in large numbers or entirely; in either case the number will be innumerable. And this means the spirits will lose their worshippers, and the number of these will also be innumerable.

Why then does the government deprive the people of their opportunities and benefits to such a great extent? It has been answered: "I covet the fame of the victor and the possessions obtainable through the conquest. So I do it."

This teaching from the Jewish text the Mishnah, which is part of the Talmud, refers to the creation of Adam, the first human.

Therefore was a single human being created: to teach you that to destroy a single human soul is equivalent to destroying an entire world; and that to sustain a single human soul is equivalent to sustaining an entire world. And a single human being was created to keep peace among human beings, that no one might say to another: My lineage is greater than yours!

(Quoted in *Gates of Repentance*)

A leading proponent of women's rights in the Islamic world, Mahnaz Afkhami was born in Iran. She is president of Women's Learning Partnership and executive director of the Foundation for Iranian Studies.

The century just passed was marked by unprecedented violence and cruelty. Most nations suffered or contributed to war, destruction, and genocide, the most egregious of which—the two world wars and the Holocaust—began and occurred mainly in the West. Untold numbers were sacrificed at the altar of ideology, religion, or ethnicity. Innocent people were led in droves to destruction in various gulags—prisons large enough to pass for cities and cities confined enough to pass for prisons.

Women and children everywhere suffered most from violence not of their making, perpetrated against them in national wars, in ethnic animosities, in petty neighborhood fights, and at home. Many of us have lived most of our lives under the threat of total annihilation because mankind achieved the technological know-how to self-destruct. . . .

As we move into the twenty-first century, women's status in society will become the standard by which to measure our progress toward civility and peace. The connection between women's human rights, gender equality, socioeconomic development, and peace is increasingly apparent.

International political and economic organizations invariably state in their official publications that achieving sustainable development in the global South, or in less-developed areas within the industrialized countries, is unlikely without women's participation. It is essential for the development of civil society, which, in turn, encourages peaceful relationships within and between societies. In other words, women, who are a majority of the peoples of the earth, are indispensable to the accumulation of the kind of social capital that is conducive to development, peace, justice, and civility.

Unless women are empowered, however, to participate in the decision-making processes—that is, unless women gain political power—it is unlikely that they will influence the economy and society toward more equitable and peaceful foundations.

(From Collopy, ed., *Architects of Peace*)

Tenzin Gyatso, the fourteenth Dalai Lama, has written many books on Buddhist principles and is a tireless advocate for peace.

In olden times when there was a war, it was a human-to-human confrontation. The victor in battle would directly see the blood and suffering of the defeated enemy.

Nowadays, it is much more terrifying because a man in an office can push a button and kill millions of people and never see the human tragedy he has created.

The mechanization of war, the mechanization of human conflict, poses an increasing threat to peace.

(*Ocean of Wisdom*)

The "Days of Awe" in the Jewish calendar are those near the holy celebration of Yom Kippur, a time of atonement for one's sins.

O Source of Peace, lead us to peace, a peace profound and true;
lead us to a healing, to mastery of all that drives us to war
within ourselves and with others.
May our deeds inscribe us in the Book of life and blessing, righteousness and peace!
O Source of Peace, bless us with peace.

(from Stern, ed., *Gates of Repentance*)

The most widely known of all Buddhist sacred writings, the Dhammapada (240 BCE) is an anthology of sayings that was written first in verse by an unknown poet. It is used as a textbook for young monks even today. This selection is entitled "Punishment."

A man is not just if he carries a matter by violence; no, he who distinguishes both right and wrong, who is learned and guides others, not by violence, but by the same law, being a guardian of the law and intelligent, he is called just.

A man is not learned because he talks much; he who is patient, free from hatred and fear, he is called learned.

James was one of the twelve apostles who followed Jesus of Nazareth and one of six considered authors of books in the Christian New Testament.

From whence come wars and fightings among you? come they not hence, even of your lusts [cravings] that war in your members? Ye lust and have not: ye kill, and desire to have, and cannot obtain: ye fight and war, yet ye have not, because ye ask not. Ye ask, and receive not, because ye ask amiss, that ye may consume it upon your lusts. Ye adulterers and adulteresses [those who break the covenant with God], know ye not that the friendship of the world is enmity with God? Whosoever therefore will be a friend of the world is the enemy of God. Do ye think that the scripture saith in vain, the spirit that dwelleth in us lusteth to envy? But he giveth more grace. Wherefore he saith, God resisteth the proud, but giveth grace unto the humble. Submit yourselves therefore to God.

(Holy Bible, the Christian Scriptures, James 4:1–7)

An early follower of Lao Tzu, founder of Taoism, Chuang-tzu (fourth century BCE) was one of the earliest sages to speak out for pacifism in warring China. This text describes him and his followers.

They sought to unite men through an ardent love in universal brotherhood. To fight against lusts and evil desires was their chief endeavor. When they were reviled, they did not consider it a shame: they were intent on nothing but the redemption of men from quarrelling. They forbade aggression, and preached disarmament in order to redeem mankind from war. This teaching they carried throughout the world. They admonished princes and instructed subjects. The world was not ready to accept their teaching, but they held to it all the more firmly. It was said that high and low tried to avoid meeting them, but that they forced themselves on peace.

(The Chuang-tzu)

Entitled "Mother in Wartime," this selection by poet and playwright Langston Hughes (1902–1967) demonstrates that he was the most versatile writer to come out of the Harlem Renaissance of New York City in the 1930s.

As if it were some noble thing,
She spoke of sons at war,
As if freedom's cause
Were pled anew at some heroic bar,
As if the weapons used today
Killed with great élan,
As if technicolor banners flew
To honor modern man—
Believing everything she read
In the daily news,
(No in-between to choose)
She thought that only
One side won,
Not that *both*
Might lose.

(The Collected Poems of Langston Hughes)

These words are excerpted from an article by journalist Somini Sengupta entitled "In the Mud, Liberia's Gentlest Rebels Pray for Peace" for The New York Times *in July, 2003. The women had a daily vigil in the field to ask God to end the terrible civil wars in their country that had lasted off and on for forty years.*

"We are tired, we are tired, we are tired of suffering," declared Louise M. Tucolon, 42 (interviewed with other Christian and Muslim women gathered for a vigil in a muddy field outside of Monrovia, Liberia during a brutal civil war). "So we come in the rain, we come in the sun to pray to our God. We know he will not come down. But he will pass through people to help us. We want this oppression of women to stop in our country. What is going on now, this raping, this abduction of our children, these are the reasons we are on the street. Tell our international brothers to come quickly," Ms. Tucolon said. "Even if right now, as I am speaking, if they could hear us, and come right now, right now, we would be happy."

The softly dancing, white-clad women with up-raised arms sing with a leader:

"Thank you, Jehovah, God, thank you, for you have spared my life to see this day."

"Liberian mothers thank you."

"Thank you, Jehovah, God, thank you."

"Thank you for intervention."

"Thank you, Jehovah, God, thank you."

Then they all sing the anthem of the civil rights movement in America, "We Shall Overcome."

A Sunday School teacher in his hometown in Georgia, former U.S. President Jimmy Carter and his wife, Rosalynn, founded the Carter Center, a nonprofit organization to promote peace, democracy, and human rights. He received the Nobel Peace Prize in 2002

It is sobering that, even in the richest nation on earth, many do not enjoy these fruits of peace. This is even more evident in the developing world. At the beginning of this century, the ratio between per capita income between the richest and poorest nations was nine to one. By 1960, it had increased to thirty to one, and today it is more than sixty to one. Although capitalism and democracy are the best ways to promote these values, these systems are far from perfect. They can promote survival of the fittest—with serious consequences to the poor—if there is little social conscience or inadequate safety nets.

There is little doubt that most people, as individuals and as a society, want to lead lives that are satisfying, productive, and healthy. To make this possible, a nation or society must reach for justice. This includes providing for the basic human needs of both the rich and the poor. Until we meet this challenge as a global community, there can be no true and lasting peace.

(Quoted in Collopy, ed., *Architects of Peace*)

The Declaration on a Culture of Peace was requested by UNESCO during its meeting in Africa in 1989 and passed by the General Assembly a few months later. The following are some excerpts.

This declaration should serve so that governments, international organizations and civil society may be guided in their activity by its provisions to promote and strengthen a Culture of Peace in the New Millennium.

ARTICLE 1: A culture of peace is a set of values, attitudes, traditions and modes of behavior and ways of life based on:

(a) Respect for life, ending of violence and promotion and practice of nonviolence through education, dialogue and cooperation;

(b) Full respect for the principles of sovereignty. . . . and non-intervention in matters which are essentially within the domestic jurisdiction of any State. . . ;

(c) Full respect for and promotion of all human rights and fundamental freedoms;

(d) Commitment to peaceful settlement of conflicts;

(e) Efforts to meet the developmental and environmental needs of present and future generations;

(f) Respect for and promotion of the right to development;

(g) Respect for and promotion of equal rights of and opportunities for women and men;

(h) Respect for and promotion of the rights of everyone to freedom of expression, opinion and information;

(i) Adherence to the principles of freedom, justice, democracy, tolerance, solidarity, cooperation, pluralism, cultural diversity, dialogue and understanding at all levels of society and among nations; and fostered by an enabling national and international environment conducive to peace. . . .

This famous anthem and widely used hymn is set to a tone poem of the same name by Finnish composer Jean Sibelius in 1899. These stanzas were first written in 1934, between the two world wars, expressing the hope of a war-weary people for peace among all lands.

Finlandia
This is my song, O God of all the nations,
    a song of peace for lands afar and mine.
This is my home, the country where my heart is;
    here are my hopes, my dreams, my holy shrine;
But other hearts in other lands are beating
    with hopes and dreams as true and high as mine.

My country's skies are bluer than the ocean,
    and sunlight beams on cloverleaf and pine;
But other lands have sunlight, too, and clover,
    and skies are everywhere as blue as mine.
O hear my song, O God of all the nations,
    a song of peace for their land and for mine.

The Rev. Dr. Martin Luther King Jr. (1929–1968), a champion of civil rights in America, said these words during his acceptance speech for the Nobel Peace Prize in 1964. The chairman of the Norwegian Nobel Committee declared: "He is the first person in the Western world to have shown us that a struggle can be waged without violence. He is the first to make the message of brotherly love a reality in the course of his struggle, and he has brought this message to all men, to all nations and races."

All that I have said boils down to the point of affirming that mankind's survival is dependent upon man's ability to solve the problems of racial injustice, poverty, and war; the solution of these problems is in turn dependent upon man's squaring his moral progress with his scientific progress, and learning the practical art of living in harmony.

For the last ten years of his life, Father Henri Nouwen (1932–1996), a Dutch-born Roman Catholic priest, ministered to developmentally

disabled residents at L'Arche Daybreak near Toronto, Canada. He was a Harvard professor, writer, spiritual leader, and activist on behalf of the poor throughout the world.

Dear Lord, awaken the people of the earth and their leaders to the realization of the madness of the nuclear arms race. Today we mourn the dead of past wars, but will there be anyone to mourn the dead of the next one?

Lord, turn us away from our foolish race to self-destruction; let us see that more and more weaponry indeed means more of a chance to use it.

Please, Lord, let the great talents you have given to your creatures not fall into the hands of the powers and principalities for whom death is the means as well as the goal. Let us see that the resources hidden in your earth are for feeding each other, healing each other, offering shelter to each other, making this world a place where men, women, and children of all races and nations can live together in peace. Give us new prophets who can speak openly, directly, convincingly, and lovingly to kings, presidents, senators, church leaders, and all men and women of good will, prophets who can make us wage peace instead of war. Lord, make haste to help us. Do not come too late! Amen.

(A Cry for Mercy)

French poet Arthur Rimbaud (1854–1891) lived a desolate life in many countries with what is described as an extreme sensibility to the "deep and eternal wound" inflicted by life and, especially, war. He used poetry for "mystic release." In this poem, "Asleep in the Valley," Rimbaud contrasts the beauty of nature with the ultimate reality of war.

A small green valley where a slow stream runs
And leaves long strands of silver on the bright
Grass; from the mountaintop stream the sun's
Rays; they fill the hollow full of light.

A soldier, very young, lies open-mouthed.
A pillow made of ferns beneath his head,
Asleep; stretched in the heavy undergrowth,
Pale in his green, warm, sun-soaked bed.

His feet among the flowers, he sleeps. His smile
Is like an infant's—gentle, without guile.
Ah, Nature, keep him warm; he may catch cold.

The humming insects don't disturb his rest;
He sleeps in sunlight, one hand on his breast,
At peace. In his side there are two red holes.

*Worldwide spiritual leader Sant Rajinder Singh Ji Maharaj said this
prayer before the Millennium World Peace Summit of Religious and
Spiritual Leaders at the United Nations in August 2000.*

May we bury our weapons of war
So they may be transformed into flowers of tranquility and bliss;
May we lay down our arms
To lift up our arms to the Creator.
May our prayers and meditation transform this world
Into a garden of everlasting joy;
And may each of us spread Light and love,
Bringing peace to the whole world.

Shinto, the native religion of ancient Japan and the official imperial religion between 1868 and 1946, now has many branches. Purification rites performed by priests are essential to Shinto beliefs and its many sanctuaries are dedicated to the kami, manifestations of the sacred.

Ten Negative Precepts of Shinto

1. Do not transgress the will of the gods.
2. Do not forget your obligations to ancestors.
3. Do not transgress the decrees of the state.
4. Do not forget the profound goodness of the gods, whereby misfortune is avoided and sickness is healed.
5. Do not forget the world is one great family.
6. Do not forget the limitations of your own person.
7. Even though others become angry, do not become angry yourself.
8. Do not be slothful in your business.
9. Do not be a person who brings blame to the teaching.
10. Do not be carried away by foreign teachings.

(Ancient Precepts of Jyegasu [Nikko, Japan])

Gadahar Ramakrishna (1836–1886) was a Bengali Hindu mystic and advocate of the unity of all religions founded in mystical experience. His follower Swami Vivekananda founded the Ramakrishna Mission movement at the first Parliament of the World's Religions in Chicago in 1893. In this text, Ramakrishna addressed the plurality of religions throughout the world.

As one can ascend to the top of a house by means of a ladder or a bamboo or a staircase or a rope, so diverse are the ways and means to approach God, and every religion in the world shows one of these ways.

Different creeds are but different paths to reach the Almighty. Various and different are the ways that lead to the temple of Mother Kali at Kalighat (Calcutta). Similarly, various are the ways that lead to the house of the Lord. Every religion is nothing but one of such paths that lead to God.

This prayer was offered by Pope John Paul II (1920–2005) during his visit to Hiroshima, Japan, in 1981, site of the first atomic bomb explosion during World War II. This first Polish Pope, consecrated in Rome in 1978, traveled the world to speak passionately against violence and wars, and passionately for justice and economic equity for all people.

To you, Creator of nature and humanity, in truth and beauty I pray:

Hear my voice, for it is the voice of victims of all wars and violence among individuals and nations,

Hear my voice, for it is the voice of all children who suffer and will suffer when people put their faith in weapons and war.

Hear my voice when I beg you to instill into the hearts of all human beings the wisdom of peace, the strength of justice and the joy of fellowship.

Hear my voice, for I speak for the multitudes in every country and every period of history who do not want war and are ready to walk the road of peace.

Hear my voice and grant insight and strength so that we may always respond to hatred with love, to injustice with total dedication to justice, to need with the sharing of self, to war with peace.

O God, hear my voice and grant unto the world your everlasting peace.

This statement by the Dalai Lama had its origin at the Parliament of the World's Religions in 1993. Winner of the Nobel Peace Prize in 1989, the Dalai Lama is leader of all Tibetan Buddhists.

Religious groups throughout the world have a responsibility to promote peace in our own age and in the future. It is true that in the history of the human family people of various religions, sometimes even acting officially in the name of their different traditions, have initiated or collaborated in systemic violence or war. At times such actions have been directed at people of other faiths or communities, as well as a particular religious denomination. This kind of behavior is totally inappropriate for spiritual persons or communities.

It is therefore time for those of us who belong to religious traditions to declare that religion can no longer be an accomplice to war, to terrorism, or to any other forms of violence, organized or spontaneous, against any member of our human family. Because this family is one, our actions must be consistent with this identity of oneness. We have an obligation to promote a new vision of society, one in which war has no place in resolving disputes among states, communities or religions, but in which nonviolence is the preeminent value in all human relations.

(Quoted in Teasdale, ed., *Community of Religions*)

Two thousand representatives of the religions of the world convened in an historic Millennium World Peace Summit of Religious and Spiritual Leaders at the United Nations in August 2000. Buddhist monks, Muslim muftis, Jewish rabbis, Hindu swamis, Christian prelates, Shinto and Zoroastrian priests, Jain and Sikh Holinesses, Traditional Religion Faithkeepers, and a Baha'i Secretary-General, among many others, brought greetings and this "Commitment to Global Peace."

We, as religious and spiritual leaders, pledge our commitment to work together to promote the inner and outer conditions that foster peace and the nonviolent management and resolution of conflict. We appeal to the followers of all religious traditions and to the human community as a whole to cooperate in building peaceful societies, to seek mutual understanding through dialogue where there are differences, to refrain from violence, to practice compassion, and to uphold the dignity of all life.

Among indigenous peoples, songs come out of the oral tradition—out of experiences the community deeply feels and that some unknown poet puts into memorable words easily sung or chanted. The source of such songs seldom can be determined, but they represent a communal spirit maintained to the present day.

Let there be peace, O son—let not war prevail.
Put down thy spear and leave it as a token—
That thy posterity may behold it.
Go to thy grandparent—to Auruia,
That he may instruct thee in the korero.

Let there be no war; for a man of war can ne'er be satiated;
But let my son be instead a man of wisdom and learning,
A keeper of the traditions of his house.
Let there be no war.
Plant deeply the spirit of peace

That your rule may be known—
    the land of all-encompassing peace.
                 (A song from Rarotonga Island, Polynesia)

The ancient Chinese sage Mo-tzu (second century BCE) reflects on the will of Heaven in this excerpt from his writings. Mo-tzu taught universal love as the central doctrine for all life.

Now, what does Heaven desire and what does it abominate? Heaven desires righteousness and abominates unrighteousness. . . . But how do we know Heaven desires righteousness and abominates unrighteousness? For, with righteousness the world lives and without it the world dies; with it the world becomes rich and without it the world becomes poor; with it the world becomes orderly and without it the world becomes chaotic. And Heaven likes to have the world live and dislikes to have it die, likes to have it rich and dislikes to have it poor, and likes to have it orderly and dislikes to have it disorderly. Therefore we know Heaven desires righteousness and abominates unrighteousness. . . .

    To obey the will of Heaven is to accept righteousness as the standard. To oppose the will of Heaven is to accept force as the standard. Now what will the standard of righteousness do?

Mo-ti said: He who rules a large state does not attack small states: he who rules a large house does not molest small houses. The strong does not plunder the weak. The honoured does not disdain the humble. The clever does not deceive the stupid. This is beneficial to Heaven above, beneficial to the spirits in the middle sphere, and beneficial to the people below. Being beneficial to these three it is beneficial to all. So the most excellent name is attributed to such a man and he is called sage-king.

(Quoted in Yutang, *The Wisdom of China and India*)

Theravada Buddhism's most ancient scriptures, of which the Vinaya Pitaka (sixth century BCE) is one, were originally in Pali, a language of India at the time these teachings of the Buddha were recorded.

A truth-finder, laying aside cudgel and sword,
     lives a life of innocence and mercy,
full of kindliness and compassion for
everything that lives.

He heals divisions, and cements friendship;
  Seeking peace, and ensuing it;
For, in peace is his delight, and his words
  Are ever the words of a peacemaker.

(Vinaya Pitaka, 5.20.1)

Born in Ilford, England, Denise Levertov (1923–1997) spent the years of World War II as a nurse in London—an experience leading to a lifetime of antiwar activism. Author and poet, she published twenty books. She taught at major universities in the United States and was arrested for a brief time in San Francisco after demonstrating against nuclear arms. This is her poem "Making Peace."

A voice from the dark called out,
  "The poets must give us imagination of peace,
  to oust the intense, familiar imagination of disaster.
  Peace, not only the absence of war."
    But peace, like a poem
is not there ahead of itself,
can't be imagined before it is made,

can't be known except in the words of its making,
grammar of justice,
syntax of mutual aid.
          A feeling towards it,
dimly sensing a rhythm, is all we have
until we begin to utter its metaphors,
learning them as we speak.
          A line of peace might appear
if we restructured the sentence our lives are making,
revoked its reaffirmation of profit and power,
questioned our needs, allowed
long pauses. . .
          A cadence of peace might balance its weight
on that different fulcrum; peace, a presence,
an energy field more intense than war,
might pulse then,
stanza by stanza into the world,
each act of living
one of its words, each word
a vibration of light—facets
of the forming crystal.

This prayer was offered by the widely quoted Baptist preacher Harry Emerson Fosdick (1878–1969). Fosdick was the famed pastor of Riverside Church in New York City from 1930 until 1946, through the Great Depression and the Second World War. He also taught practical theology at the nearby Union Theological Seminary.

Eternal God, Father of all souls, grant unto us such clear vision of the sin of war, such hearty hatred for the passions which create it and for the desolations which follow it, that we may earnestly desire and tirelessly seek that co-operation between nations which alone can make war impossible.

As we by our inventions have made the whole world into one neighborhood, grant that we may not fail by co-operations to make the world into one neighborhood.

Break down all race prejudice, all ignoble narrowness in national loyalty; stay the greed of those who profit by war and the ambitions of those who by imperialistic conquest seek a national greatness which, drenched in blood, cannot endure; guide all leaders who seek a just basis for international action in the interests of peace.

Along with the United Nations itself, UNESCO was formed soon after the end of World War II in recognition of the need for cultural exchanges as well as political dialogues for world peace to be a possibility in the future. Its headquarters is in Paris, France, and its branches and projects are in nearly every country of the world. This is an excerpt from UNESCO's Constitution, written in 1945.

The Governments of the States Parties to this Constitution on behalf of their peoples declare:

That since wars begin in the minds of human beings, it is in the minds of human beings that the defenses of peace must be constructed;

That ignorance of each other's ways and lives has been a common cause, throughout the history of humankind, of that suspicion and mistrust between the peoples of the world through which their differences have all too often broken into war; . . . .

That a peace based exclusively upon the political and economic arrangements of governments would not be a peace which could secure the unanimous, lasting and sincere support of the peoples of the world, and that the peace must therefore be founded, if it is not to fail, upon the intellectual and moral solidarity of humankind.

For these reasons, the States Parties to this Constitution, believing in full and equal opportunities for education for all, in the unrestricted pursuit of objective truth, and in the free exchange of ideas and knowledge, are agreed and determined to develop and to increase the means of communication between their peoples and to employ these means for the purposes of mutual understanding and a truer and more perfect knowledge of each other's lives. . . .

In consequence whereof they do hereby create the United Nations Educational, Scientific and Cultural Organization for the purpose of advancing, through the educational and scientific and cultural relations of the peoples of the world, the objectives of international peace and of the common welfare of humankind for which the United Nations Organization was established and which its Charter proclaims.

Born in 1941 in Costa Rica, Oscar Arias Sánchez is a former president of that country and a Nobel laureate in 1987 for his Arias Peace Initiative for the Central American region. These words of Arias are excerpted from an address he gave at the International Peace Conference in Munich in 1999.

. . . It is imperative that governments, civil society actors and ordinary citizens make a collective re-commitment to the basic values that give peace meaning: compassion, tolerance and justice. For, as the martyred Salvadoran Bishop Oscar Romero once said, "The only peace that God wants is a peace based in justice." Remembering his words, we must not work only to silence the guns. We must dedicate ourselves to silencing the cries of the excluded, the hungry, and the oppressed. It is only then that the beautiful words of peace will ring true for all but a privileged minority of our human community. And it is only through a personal commitment from each of us that the foundations of a new culture will be laid: a culture which celebrates peace as a way of life.

The Nuer tribespeople of East Africa believe that prayer is appropriate anytime they are happy, so their traditional prayers, such as the one here, can be spoken frequently. This text was used at the Inter Religious Federation for World Peace Congress in New Delhi, India, 1993.

Our Father, it is thy universe, it is thy will,
    let us be at peace,
Let the soul of thy people be cool.
Thou art our Father,
Remove all evil from our path.

American astronaut Russell Schweickart wrote these words in 1977, later used in a booklet prepared by a group called Beyond War. An aeronautical engineer and pilot, Schweickart became an astronaut in 1963 and logged 241 hours in space.

When you go around the Earth in an hour and a half, you begin to recognize that your identity is with that whole thing. And that makes a change.

You look down there and you can't imagine how many borders and boundaries you cross, again and again and again, and you don't even see them. There you are—hundreds of people in the Mid-East killing each other over some imaginary line that you're not even aware of, that you can't see. And from where you see it, the thing is a whole, and it's so beautiful. You wish you could take one in each hand, one from each side in the various conflicts, and say, "Look. Look at it from this perspective. Look at that. What's important?"

And a little later on, your friend, again one of those same neighbors, the person next to you, goes out to the moon. And now he looks back and he sees the Earth not as something big, where he can see the beautiful details, but now he sees the Earth as a small thing out there. And the contrast between that bright blue and white Christmas tree ornament and the black sky, that infinite universe, really comes through, and the size of it, the significance of it. It is so small and so fragile and such a precious little spot in that universe that you can block it out with your thumb, and you realize that on that small spot, that little blue and white thing, is everything that means anything to you—all of history and music and poetry and art and death and birth and love, tears, joy, games, all of it on that little spot out there that you can cover with your thumb. And you realize from that perspective that you've changed, that there's something new there, that the relationship is no longer what it was.

This prayer is from the "Concluding Service" of a collection of prayers for the Jewish "Days of Awe," or Yom Kippur.

Everlasting God, we turn now to You once more to cry out
    our longing and the longing of all men and women for a
    beginning of that wholeness we call peace. Ever and again,
    we now admit, we have turned our backs on You, and on
    our sisters and brothers: forsaking Your Law, denying Your
    truth, ignoring Your will, defacing Your beauty. The
    intelligence You have implanted within us we have applied
    to the arts of war; with the skill we have from You we
    make engines of terror and pain.
We have prayed for peace, even as we laughed at truth; for

blessing, but did not care to do Your will; for mercy, and
have shown none to others. We have prayed for impossible
things: peace without justice, forgiveness without restitution,
love without sacrifice.

But You, our Maker, abound in grace: so now again we turn to
You, to attach ourselves to Your purpose, to set ourselves
on the paths that lead to the coming of peace and right,
freedom and joy for Israel and all the world.

Again, as the shadows fall, we ask forgiveness, and again we
praise You, O God, the Source of peace.

(From Stern, ed., *Gates of Repentance*)

Known throughout the world for her compassionate work with the destitute of Calcutta, India, Mother Teresa (1910–1997) founded the Roman Catholic Missionaries of Charity to help those dying in poverty in 500 locations around the world.

The fruit of silence is prayer;
The fruit of prayer is faith;
The fruit of faith is love;

The fruit of love is service;
The fruit of service is peace.

(Quoted in Collopy, ed., Architects of Peace)

This is one of several similar prayers devout Hindus can chant on appropriate occasions. Scholars report that the oft-repeated term "all" in prayers like this refers to everyone in the world to illustrate the interdependence of the welfare of one with the welfare of all.

May there be welfare to all beings; may there be fullness and
    wholeness to all people;
May there be constant good and auspicious life to everyone; may
    there be peace everywhere. . . .
May all be full of happiness and abundance; may everyone in the
    world enjoy complete health, free from diseases;
May all see and experience good things in their lives, may not
    even a single person experience sorrow and misery. Om!
Peace! Peace! Peace!

Partial Bibliography

Ballou, Robert O., ed. *The Portable World Bible.* New York: Penguin Books, 1944.

Beversluis, Joel. *Sourcebook of the World's Religions: An Interfaith Guide to Religion and Spirituality.* Novato, CA: New World Library, 2000.

Birnbaum, Philip. *A Treasury of Judaism.* New York: Hebrew Publishing Company, 1957.

Browne, Lewis. *The World's Great Scriptures: An Anthology of the Sacred Books of the Ten Principal Religions.* New York: The Macmillan Company, 1946.

Champion, Selwyn Gurney, and Dorothy Short, eds. *Readings from World Religions.* London: Watts & Co., 1952.

Cleary, Thomas. *The Essential Koran: The Heart of Islam.* HarperSanFrancisco, 1993.

Collopy, Michael, ed. *Architects of Peace: Visions of Hope in Words and Images*. Novato, CA: New World Library, 2000.

Craughwell, Thomas J., ed. *Every Eye Beholds You: A World Treasury of Prayer*. Introduction by Karen Armstrong. New York: Harcourt Brace & Co., 1998.

Cuomo, Kerry Kennedy, and Nan Richardson, eds., and Eddie Adams, photographer. *Speak Truth to Power: Human Rights Defenders Who Are Changing Our World*. New York: Crown Publishers, 2000.

Dalai Lama. *Kindness, Clarity and Insight*. Ithaca, NY: Snow Lion Publications, 1984.

———. *Ocean of Wisdom: Guidelines for Living*. San Francisco: Harper, 1990.

Eiseley, Loren C. *All the Strange Hours: The Excavation of a Life*. New York: Scribner's, 1975.

Eliade, Mircea, and Joan P. Couliano with Hillary S. Wiesner. *The HarperCollins Concise Guide to World Religions*. New York: HarperCollins, 1991.

Ellul, Jacques. *Prayer and Modern Man*. Seabury Press, 1973.

Fahey, Joseph J., and Richard Armstrong, eds. *A Peace Reader: Essential Readings on War, Justice, Non-Violence and World Order*. Mahwah, NJ: Paulist Press, 1992.

Ferguson, John. *War and Peace in the World's Religions*. New York: Oxford University Press, 1978.

Ford-Grabowsky, Mary. *Prayers for All People*. New York: Doubleday, 1995.

Griffiths, Bede. *Universal Wisdom: A Journey Through the Sacred Wisdom of the World*. New York: HarperCollins, 1994.

Hedges, Chris. *War Is a Force that Gives Us Meaning*. New York: Public Affairs, 2002.

Holy Bible. Hebrew Scriptures: Jewish sacred scripture consists primarily of works called "The Law, Prophets, and Writings." Part of the most ancient of these, the Torah, or Pentateuch ("five writings"), is dated to the tenth century BCE; the most recent of the other writings of the Hebrew Scriptures are dated to the second century BCE, when the first collection of biblical texts was created in the Greek language. Scrolls of the Torah, usually in the Hebrew language, are often kept in the front of contemporary Jewish synagogues.

Christian Scriptures: The final collection of twenty-seven writings by early Christians, called the New Testament, was approved in the fourth century CE and is increasingly known today as the Christian scriptures. Church leaders and translators at that time also included the Jewish scriptures, called the Old Testament, in its completed Holy Bible. The most ancient part of Christian scriptures, the authentic letters of Paul of Tarsus, is dated c. 50–60 CE.

Hughes, Langston. *The Collected Poems of Langston Hughes*. New York: Alfred A. Knopf, 1994.

Hume, Robert Ernest. *Treasure-House of the Living Religions*. New York: Charles Scribner's Sons, 1932.

International Religious Foundation. *World Scripture: A Comparative Anthology of Sacred Texts*. New York: Paragon House, 1991.

Kome, Penney, and Patrick Crean, eds. *Peace: A Dream Unfolding*. San Francisco, CA: Sierra Club Books, 1986.

Leadingham, Carrie, Joann E. Moschella, and Hilary M. Vartanian, eds. *Peace Prayers: Meditations, Affirmations, Invocations, Poems, and Prayers for Peace*. HarperSanFrancisco, 1992.

Lesher, A. Jean, ed. *Prayers for the Common Good*. Cleveland, OH: The Pilgrim Press, 1998.

Mead, Margaret. *World Enough: Rethinking the Future*. Boston: Little, Brown and Company, 1975.

Nhat Hanh, Thích. *Living Buddha, Living Christ*. New York: Riverhead Books, 1995.

———. *Call Me By My True Names*. Berkeley, CA: Parallax Press, 1993.

Nouwen, Henri. *A Cry for Mercy: Prayers from the Genesee*. New York: Doubleday, 1981.

Novak, Philip. *The World's Wisdom: Sacred Texts of the World's Religions*. HarperSanFrancisco, 1994.

Potter, Jean, and Marcus Braybrooke, eds. *All in Good Faith: A Resource Book for Multi-Faith Prayer*. Oxford, GB: The World Congress of Faiths, 1997.

Rausch, David A., and Carl Hermann Voss. *World Religions: Our Quest for Meaning*. Minneapolis: Fortress Press, 1989.

Sharma, Arvind, ed. *Our Religions*. HarperSanFrancisco, 1993.

Smith, Huston. *The World's Religions: Our Great Wisdom Traditions*. HarperSanFrancisco, 1991.

Star, Jonathan. *Two Suns Rising: A Collection of Sacred Writings*. New York: Bantam Books, 1991.

Stern, Chaim. *Gates of Repentance: The New Union Prayerbook for the Days of Awe*. New York: Central Conference of American Rabbis, 1999.

Teasdale, Wayne, and George Cairns, eds. *Community of Religions: Voices and Images of the Parliament of the World's Religions*. New York: Continuum, 1996.

Tillich, Paul. *Theology of Peace*. Lousiville, KY: Westminster John Knox Press, 1990.

Wiesel, Elie. *And the Sea Is Never Full: Memoirs 1969–*. New York: Alfred A. Knopf, 1999.

Yutang, Lin. *The Wisdom of China and India*. New York: Modern Library, 1955.

Index of Authors and Titles